International
Library of the
Philosophy of
Education

**Education and the
education of
teachers**

International
Library of the
Philosophy of
Education

General Editor

R. S. Peters

**Professor of Philosophy of Education
Institute of Education
University of London**

Education and the education of teachers

R. S. Peters

Professor of Philosophy of Education
Institute of Education
University of London

Routledge & Kegan Paul

London, Henley and Boston

First published in 1977
by Routledge & Kegan Paul Ltd
39 Store Street,
London WC1E 7DD,
Broadway House,
Newtown Road,
Henley-on-Thames,
Oxon RG9 1EN and
9 Park Street,
Boston, Mass. 02108, USA
Set in IBM Baskerville
by Express Litho Service, Oxford,
and printed in Great Britain by
Redwood Burn Ltd
Trowbridge and Esher

ISBN 0 7100 8469 2

Contents

General editor's note

There is a growing interest in philosophy of education amongst students of philosophy as well as amongst those who are more specifically and practically concerned with educational problems. Philosophers, of course, from the time of Plato onwards, have taken an interest in education and have dealt with education in the context of wider concerns about knowledge and the good life. But it is only quite recently in this country that philosophy of education has come to be conceived of as a specific branch of philosophy like the philosophy of science or political philosophy.

To call philosophy of education a specific branch of philosophy is not, however, to suggest that it is a distinct branch in the sense that it could exist apart from established branches of philosophy such as epistemology, ethics, and philosophy of mind. It would be more appropriate to conceive of it as drawing on established branches of philosophy and bringing them together in ways which are relevant to educational issues. In this respect the analogy with political philosophy would be a good one. Thus use can often be made of work that already exists in philosophy. In tackling, for instance, issues such as the rights of parents and children, punishment in schools, and the authority of the teacher, it is possible to draw on and develop work already done by philosophers on 'rights', 'punishment', and 'authority'. In other cases, however, no systematic work exists in the relevant branches of philosophy — e.g. on concepts such as 'education', 'teaching', 'learning', 'indoctrination'. So philosophers of education have had to break new ground — in these cases in the philosophy of mind. Work on educational issues can also bring to life and throw new light on long-standing problems in philosophy. Concentration, for instance, on the particular predicament of children can throw new light on problems of punishment and responsibility. G. E. Moore's old worries about what sorts of things are good in themselves can be brought to life by urgent questions about the justification of the curriculum in schools.

There is a danger in philosophy of education, as in any other applied field, of polarization to one of two extremes. The work could be practically relevant but philosophically feeble; or it could be philosophically sophisticated but remote from practical problems. The aim of the new International Library of the Philosophy of Education is to build up a body of fundamental work in this area which is both practically relevant and philosophically competent. For unless it achieves both types of objective it will fail to satisfy those for whom it is intended and fall short of the conception of philosophy of education which the International Library is meant to embody.

R.S.P.

Acknowledgments

I am grateful to the editors and publishers who have granted permission for the reprinting of material previously published in their books and journals.

Chapter 1: *Philosophy of Education Society of Great Britain Proceedings*, January 1970, © Basil Blackwell & Mott. Chapter 2: C. Beeby (ed.), *Qualitative Aspects of Educational Planning*, by permission of Unesco and IIEP, © Unesco 1969. Chapter 3: K. A. Strike and K. Egan, *Ethics and Educational Policy,* © Routledge & Kegan Paul Ltd, 1977. Chapter 4: paper read Department of Politics, University of Hull, 1973, © R. S. Peters, 1977. Chapter 5: R. S. Peters (ed.), *The Philosophy of Education,* © Oxford University Press, 1973. Chapter 6: © *Didaskalos,* vol. 5, no. 1, 1975. Chapter 7: ATCDE-DES Conference, Hull, 1964, © R. S. Peters, 1964. Chapter 8: ATCDE-DES Conference, Avery Hill College, 1967, © R. S. Peters, 1967. Chapter 9: Standing Conference in Educational Studies, 1972, © Basil Blackwell & Mott, 1973. Chapter 10: *London Educational Review,* vol. 1, no. 1, spring 1972, © University of London Institute of Education.

Introduction

This collection of papers represents the author's developing thought over the past ten years about education and the education of teachers. The first two papers were given at conferences and represent attempts at the end of the 1960s to make clearer what might be meant by 'education' and by the 'quality of education' — a phrase that is often used in public debate — e.g. about comprehensive schools, but seldom analysed. The next two papers, dealing with liberal education, are more recent products. In the first, ambiguities are explored in the interpretation of liberal education as 'knowledge for its own sake', as general education, and as non-authoritarian education, and attention is drawn to the fact that no determinate answer is given by any of these interpretations to Herbert Spencer's question, 'What knowledge is of most worth?' In the second paper, which was first read at the Hull department of politics, the dilemmas and problems facing any teacher who is committed to liberal education, in any of its senses, are sketched. The fifth paper is a reprint of the author's attempt to improve on, as well as clarify, his first attempt to justify education in *Ethics and Education*. The sixth paper was originally given to the Joint Association of Classics Teachers, and is a constructive attempt at bringing out what is acceptable in Plato's views about education instead of concentrating on the easier and more usual task of emphasizing what is unacceptable.

The second section begins with the author's contribution to the ATCDE-DES Conference at Hull in 1964, which was a landmark in the attempt to raise standards in educational theory by differentiation of the disciplines that contribute to it. One result of this differentiation was predictable — that the disciplines would tend to go their own way, and that many educational problems would remain in as confused a state as ever because they require an interdisciplinary approach. The third paper in this section stresses the need both for such interdisciplinary work and for relating theory to practical problems. In the second paper, which was delivered at another ATCDE-DES conference in 1967, stress is placed on the role of content in the training of teachers. It is no good introducing teachers to a mass of fascinating findings and speculations in educational theory if they lack a thorough mastery of something to teach. The final paper was written at the time of the James Report when the involvement of the universities in the education of teachers was seriously threatened. It tries to set out the case for the universities maintaining this involvement. The author was at that time Dean of the Faculty of Education, and Chairman of the Board of Educational Studies of the University of London and centrally involved in the endless discussions and negotiations that followed the government's White Paper *Higher Education: A Framework for Expansion.*

It is hoped that these papers will not seem to be of purely historical interest; for they raise questions of perennial importance — e.g. about education, its quality and aims, about the content of liberal education, about the nature of educational theory and its relationship to practice, and about the role of the universities in the education of teachers. But even when looked at purely historically the papers in Part 2 are significant documents; for they reflect the rapidity of the changes which have taken place in the past ten years in teacher education. In 1964 when the Hull conference took place, the three-year course had just been introduced in the colleges. Discussion revolved around how best to use the extra year and how to raise standards. There was then the frantic period of expansion which coincided with the introduction of the B Ed degree. Now we are in a period of contraction with an emphasis on the practical and a great variety of attempts to relate theory to practice. The 1972 paper on 'Education as an Academic Discipline' reflects the developing mood of the early 1970s as much as the 1964 paper on 'The Place of Philosophy in the Training of Teachers' reflected the aspirations of the early 1960s. The interesting question for the future is whether the emphasis on theory of the 1960s will tighten up and give depth to the more practical concerns of the 1970s.

Education

part **I**

Education and the educated man[1]

Some further reflections

1 The comparison with 'reform'

In reflecting, in the past, on the sort of term that 'education' is I have usually likened it to 'reform'. Reforming people involves putting them in the way of experiences that, it is thought, will make them better. There is thus the idea of a family of processes whose principle of unity is the contribution to the very general end of being better. This is a very formal notion because 'better' has to be interpreted in terms of the valuations of the person using the term and a great number of processes might bring about the desired end. 'Education', I have argued, is a similar term, but more complex. It is similar because it suggests a family of processes whose principle of unity is the development of desirable qualities in someone. There are many processes, too, which might contribute to bringing about these valuable qualities and 'valuable' would have to be interpreted in terms of the valuations of the person, or group of people, using the word. 'Aims' of education are attempts to specify more precisely what these desirable qualities are, e.g. critical thought, integrity of character, being creative, and the like.

The differences between the two terms are, it was suggested, as follows:

(a) 'Reform' suggests that a person has lapsed from some standard of approved behaviour. 'Education', on the other hand, has no such suggestion. It often consists of putting people in the way of values of which they have never dreamt.

(b) 'Reform' suggests a limited operation. Making a boy more prudent would almost count as reforming him if he found difficulty in delaying gratification. 'Education' is not so limited. Indeed it suggests passing on some positive values of a community, so that the individual can make them his own.

(c) 'Education' suggests not only that what develops in someone is valuable but also that it involves the development of knowledge and understanding. Whatever else an educated person is, he is one who has some understanding of something. He is not just a person who has a know-how or knack. There is also the suggestion that this understanding should not be too narrowly specialized. This led me to suggest that the saying that 'education is of the whole man' is a conceptual truth in that being educated is incompatible with being narrowly specialized.

There are all sorts of further questions which arise from this analysis — e.g. about whether there are any conceptual as distinct from moral limits which could be set to what is to count as a process of education, about the ethical justification of our views about what is desirable and about what are ethically defensible methods of passing it on and distributing it. With these I am not here concerned; for I want to confine myself to asking prior questions about whether any conditions that begin to look like logically necessary conditions for the correct application of the term 'education' have been provided.

2 Objections to cognitive conditions

Counter-examples can be produced to this analysis, some of which are more difficult to deal with than others. Let us consider first some objections to the cognitive conditions:

(i) We can talk of specialized education. This objection can be met by saying that often, when we have multiple conditions, we can withdraw one of them by using a countermanding word. For instance people speak of knowing things 'intuitively', where 'intuitively' countermands one of the usual conditions of 'knowledge', namely that we have grounds for what we believe. Similarly, 'specialized' could be regarded as withdrawing one of the conditions of 'education'.

(ii) We might talk of Spartan education or of education in some even more primitive tribe when we knew that they had nothing to pass on except simple skills and folk-lore. This could be met, perhaps, by saying either that we were extending the term analogically as when we talk about dogs being neurotic (although it is interesting to note that we do not now talk of the education of animals), or that the word 'education' was being used with reliance purely on the first condition, in the sense of bringing up their children in what is thought to be valuable, or that the word 'education' was being misused. We might also note that the jobs which words do is relative to the conceptual structure of the people who employ them. For people who have not advanced to the level where they make a distinction between 'education' and 'training' or 'bringing up' one word might function in a much more undifferentiated way. And even for people who have developed a more precise way of using words the same words are sometimes used in the more general way in which they were once used. Nevertheless this counter-example is a difficult one to meet.

3 The value-condition the only one?

Some might regard this counter-example as decisive and go on to suggest a simplified analysis of the concept of 'education' along the following lines. They might argue that the value condition of 'education' is the only one which is properly speaking a logically necessary condition. The basic notion involved in 'education', it might be maintained, is that of the development of desirable qualities in people. As a matter of contingent fact we value knowledge and breadth of understanding. The supposed knowledge conditions, therefore, are not properly logical conditions of 'education' but contingent on our particular valuations. On this view an educated person would be one who pursues things that are valuable. He is a person who has become committed to a certain way of life that is valued by society and by learning he has succeeded in getting into this state. In our contemporary culture the things judged valuable are centred upon knowledge and understanding either in the sense that value is

5

attached to various forms of the pursuit of truth or in the sense that other valuable things — e.g. sex, eating, gardening, are more highly valued if they are pursued in a sensitive, discriminating or informed way. The notion, therefore, of being 'educated' has become contingently but firmly associated with knowledge and understanding. This means that, because we judge knowledge and understanding to be valuable, a concept, which in other contexts may be associated with other valuable pursuits, is for us associated with what is related to knowledge and understanding. We might have put other things of value under this concept but we have not in fact done so. Some people in our culture do, perhaps, put other things under this concept. So their concept of being educated includes things like being clean, tidy, and speaking with a nice accent. If, however, they do not regard knowledge and understanding as valuable at all, then they give quite a different content to the concept of being educated, for their values are quite different.

Let us now briefly examine the plausibility of this way of simplifying the analysis:

(i) Its strongest point is that it gets rid of the problems connected with talking about Spartan education. The Spartans had a system of values in which knowledge and understanding were not valued very highly. An educated Spartan, on this view, would not be a rarity but a Spartan who had become, by his upbringing, committed to some things that are valuable but not to knowledge and understanding.

(ii) Another argument in favour of this view is that 'education' certainly has a use in which it suggests the commitment to what is thought to be of value which has been brought about by some process of initiation. There are some, for instance, who are insensitive to the values inherent in a game like golf. Perhaps they think of it as a good walk spoilt; perhaps, because of their unfortunate upbringing, they associate it with the upper class — like polo and riding to hounds. I might well say to such a philistine that he just was not educated. If I said this I don't think I would necessarily be drawing attention to his ignorance of the history of the game, to the fact that in the country of its origin it is as much a people's game as football. What I think I would be suggesting is that he was not on the inside of it at all, that he had failed to see what there was in it. He had not been initiated. Similarly, when we say that a person has uneducated tastes, do we mean necessarily that he does not value knowledge and understanding either for their own sake or as ingredients in whatever tastes he has? Or do we mean that his tastes are, in our view, for all the wrong things?

What I think we are pointing to in cases such as these is the absence of the sort of knowledge which presented such a problem in Greek ethics — the knowledge of what is good. This consists in seeing things under certain aspects which constitute intrinsic reasons for engaging in them. It is impossible here to go into all the complications involved in this sort of knowledge. It is, as Socrates and Plato argued, intimately connected with caring about something and does not seem to be a case either of 'knowing how' or of 'knowing that' which are the usual alternatives offered. But it may well be that when we talk about people being educated we sometimes have this sort of value commitment in mind. So this sort of case would seem to support the connexion of 'education' with the value condition and its separation from the knowledge condition if the latter is just interpreted as suggesting depth and breadth of understanding.

There are, however, objections of varying degrees of seriousness not just to making the value condition the logically fundamental one but to regarding it as a logically necessary condition *at all* for the application of the term 'education'. They are as follows:

(i) We often talk of the educational system of a country without commending what others seem concerned to pass on. This objection can be met by citing the parallel of talking about the moral code of another community or of a subculture within our own. Once we understand from our own case how terms such as 'educate' and 'moral' function we can use them in an external descriptive sort of way as do anthropologists, economists and the like. We can also use them in what Hare has called a 'quotes' sense. (See Hare, 1952, pp. 124–6.)

(ii) We can talk of poor education or bad education. This

7

can be met by saying that we are suggesting that the job is being botched or that the values with which it is concerned are not up to much — though it is a nice point when we would pass from saying that it is bad education to saying that it is not education at all.

(iii) A very serious objection, however, to this way of simplifying the analysis is that many people regard being educated as a bad state to be in. Their objection is not just to a particular system of education but to *any* sort of education. Perhaps they associate it with books and theories and fail to appreciate the various ways in which knowledge can transform people's lives. Nevertheless they are contemptuous of all its manifestations ranging from literature to heart-surgery and going to the moon. They think that people are better off without it. They would not describe bringing up their children in the fear of the Lord and in the ways of their forefathers as education. So they would not, in their use of the term, retain any association between education and what they thought valuable. For them it would be connected with what others try to do to them and to their children which had some intimate connexion with knowledge. And they might not themselves have a specific concept to differentiate the handing on of what they thought valuable, let alone a specific word to mark it.

4 The cognitive conditions fundamental?

The suggestion that one condition, namely the valuative one, might be the only proper logical condition, and that the cognitive conditions might be thought of as contingent on our valuations is an ingenious one, though it is faced with the problem raised at the end which is posed by those who do not value education at all. But it might equally well be suggested that the cognitive conditions might be the only proper logical conditions and the valuative condition contingent on them.[2] This might prove to be no better and no worse a way of simplifying the analysis. On this view the fundamental notion involved in being educated would be that of having knowledge and understanding. Because knowledge and understanding are valued in our culture, both for their own sake and for what they contribute to technology and to our quality of life generally, being educated has come to be thought of as a highly desirable state to be in.

This way of simplifying the analysis has much to commend it:

(i) It certainly takes care of those who regard education as a bad thing. As, on this view, the connexion between education and something that is valued depends only on the contingent fact that people value knowledge and understanding, it is not surprising that simple people or hard-headed practical men are against it. For it seems to serve no useful function in their lives; indeed it may be seen as an influence that is likely to undermine their way of life. If they see that it may help them to run a farm or to cure a disease they may accord a limited value to it, but only of an instrumental type.

(ii) There would be no need to make any elaborate philosophical moves to deal with cases where we speak of education and educational systems without approving or disapproving of what goes on. Education would be, as indeed it is sometimes called, the 'knowledge industry'. We could talk of it in the same way as we talk of any other set of practices that we might or might not think important.

(iii) 'Poor' or 'bad' education would simply mark the efficiency with which knowledge was handed on or the worth of the type of knowledge that was handed on.

The main objection to this alternative is the fact that 'education' is, or has been, used without this conceptual connexion which is suggested with knowledge. The Latin word 'educere' was usually, though not always, used of physical development. In Silver Latin 'educare' was used of the rearing of plants and animals as well as children. In English the word was originally used just to talk in a very general way about the bringing up of children and animals. In the seventeenth century, for instance, harts were said to delight in woods and places of their first education. The word was often used of animals and birds that were trained by human beings such as hounds and falcons. In the nineteenth century it was even used of silkworms! (See *OED*.) Nowadays we sometimes use it in this general way as when, for instance, we talk about Spartan education or when we use it of our own

9

forms of training which do not have any close connexion with knowledge and understanding. In other words the older use still survives.

Arguments from etymology, of course, establish very little. At best they provide clues which it may be worth while to follow up. In this case, for instance, it seems that the word originally had a very generalized meaning. With the coming of industrialism, however, and the increasing demand for knowledge and skill consequent on it, 'education' became increasingly associated with 'schooling' and with the sort of training and instruction that went on in special institutions. This large-scale change, culminating in the development of compulsory schooling for all, may well have brought about such a radical conceptual tightening up that we now only tend to use the word in connexion with the development of knowledge and understanding. We distinguish now between 'training' and 'education', whereas previously people did not. We would not now naturally speak of educating animals and we would never speak in this way of plants. But we do speak of training animals and of training roses and other sorts of plants.

We thus seem to have reached an impasse in our attempts to simplify the analysis, whichever way we attempt to do it. For there are considerations that pull in both directions. There is, however, another etymological point which might help to explain some of the difficulties which surround this concept and which might shed some light on how this impasse can be surmounted.

5   Education and the educated man

A little research in the *OED* reveals that the notion of 'educated' as characterizing the all-round development of a person morally, intellectually, and spiritually only emerged in the nineteenth century. It was also in this century that the distinction between education and training came to be made explicitly. This use was very much connected with instruction by means of which desirable mental qualities were thought to be produced, as well as with the drawing out and development of qualities thought to be potential in a person. The term, however, continued to be used, as it had previously been used, to refer to the rearing and bringing up of children and animals, as well as to the sort of instruction that went on in schools. In other words, though previously to the nineteenth century there had been the ideal of the cultivated person who was the product of elaborate training and instruction, the term 'an educated man' was not the usual one for drawing attention to this ideal. They had the concept but they did not use the word 'educated' quite with these overtones. Education therefore, was not thought of explicitly as a family of processes which have as their outcome the development of an educated man in the way in which it is now.

Nowadays, especially in educational circles, the concept of an educated man as an ideal has very much taken root. It is natural, therefore, for those working in educational institutions to conceive of what they are doing as being connected with the development of such a person. They have become very sensitive to the difference between working with this ideal in mind and having limited and specific goals, for which they use the word 'training'. Witness, for instance, the change in nomenclature, following the Robbins Report, from Training Colleges to Colleges of Education. Witness, too, the change from Physical Training to Physical Education. In brief, because of the development of the concept of an 'educated man', the concept of 'education' has become tightened up because of its natural association with the development of such a person. We distinguish educating people from training them because for us education is no longer compatible with any narrowly conceived enterprise.

Now in the analysis which I have previously given of 'education' as being comparable to 'reform' I have always assumed this connexion between 'education' and the development of an educated man. I have admitted that other people may not have developed this more differentiated type of conceptual structure, but I have insisted that it is important to make these distinctions even if people do not use terms in a specific enough way to mark them out. (See Peters, 1966, pp. 29–30.) But perhaps I did not appreciate how widespread the older use of 'education' is in which there is no such tight connexion between various processes of bringing up and rearing and the development of an educated man. It may well be that many people still use the word 'education' to cover not only any process of instruction, training, etc., that goes on in schools but also less formalized child-rearing practices such as toilet-training, getting children to be clean and tidy, and to speak with a nice accent. I do not think, however, that the word is now used, except semi-humorously, to talk about the training of animals, and I have never heard it used to honour the labours of gardeners with their plants. At least the concept has shifted more or less universally in these respects from that of the seventeenth century.

What light, then, does this general point derived from etymology throw on the two alternative proposals for simplifying the analysis of 'education' that were suggested? It depends, I think, whether we are concerned with the analysis of 'education' or with that of 'an educated man'. If we are concerned with the analysis of 'education', then, I think that the first alternative is the obvious one. 'Education' was originally used to mark out any process of rearing, bringing up, instructing, etc. As those who engaged in this would not have bothered had they not thought that some importance attached to what was being passed on, there must always have been some loose kind of connexion between these processes and conceptions of what was valuable. It is doubtful, however, whether at this stage the connexion could be thought of as a conceptual one; for at a stage when 'bringing up' is just one of the functions of the family and not a function of special educational institutions it is unlikely that much thought is given to what is really worth passing on and what is not. Education, therefore, must have included passing on things that were thought valuable but probably also included a lot of other things that were of little importance. With the coming of industrialism, however, an increasing value came to be placed on literacy, numeracy, knowledge, and skill; so, with the widespread development of special institutions to pass on this growing inheritance, education came to be associated very closely with the various processes of instruction which went on in such institutions. So close has this association become that it is now possible for some people, who do not value anything to do with books or theory, to say that they do not value education. Many others, however, who do value it, do not necessarily do so because they view it as leading up to the outcome of an educated man. They value it because it has now become the royal road to better jobs and to getting on in the world.

If, however, we start, as I did, from the analysis of what it means to be 'educated' and view education as the family of processes which contribute to this outcome, then the association both with knowledge and with all-round development takes over. The value condition is indissolubly connected with this; for the notion of an educated man functions as an ideal for those who view education as being concerned with the development of such a person. This ideal emerged into prominence when the importance of specialized knowledge became manifest in the nineteenth century. As a reaction against utilitarian specialization it upheld the value both of the disinterested pursuit of knowledge and of all-round understanding and development. At that time there was still prevalent amongst educated people a contempt for trade and technology. Because, too, practical pursuits, such as farming and cooking, were usually conceived of instrumentally, they were not regarded as central to the life of an educated person, though they might be indulged in as hobbies. The Greek ideal persisted of a man who was freed from coarsening contact with the materials of the earth and who developed knowledge both for its own sake and in order to control himself and other men. Once, however, especially through the influence of the romantic protest, the practical became dissociated from the instrumental, it became possible to accord intrinsic value to a range of disinterested pursuits in addition to the pursuit of knowledge. Thus our concept of an educated person is of someone who is capable of delighting in a variety of pursuits and projects for their own sake and whose pursuit of them and general conduct of his life is transformed by some degree of all round understanding and sensitivity. Pursuing the practical is not necessarily a disqualification for being educated; for the practical need not be pursued under a purely instrumental aspect. This does not mean, of course, that an educated man is oblivious to the instrumental value of pursuits — e.g. of science. It means only that he does not view them purely under this aspect. Neither does it mean that

13

he has no specialized knowledge; it only means that he is not just a narrow-minded specialist.

It is one thing to argue that, because the concept of an educated man came into prominence at a certain time as an ideal, the value condition must necessarily be satisfied; but it is quite another matter to outline the precise ways in which such an outcome is valuable. Obviously being educated is a desirable state to be in, for those for whom it functions as an ideal, because of the ways in which value can be ascribed to the pursuit and possession of knowledge — i.e. as an absorbing and challenging activity, as illuminating other pursuits, and as incorporating the intrinsic value of truth. But what is to be said, ethically speaking, about the non-instrumental aspect of being an educated man? It could be argued that value must be ascribed to this because the capacity for appreciating activities in this way is central to being on the inside of them and doing them for their own sake. But this form of appreciation would have to be distinguished from more brutish and unreflective enjoyment — e.g. of food, sex, etc. And it might be argued that the difference in levels of enjoyment is due to the presence or absence of a kind of knowledge which Plato and Socrates called 'knowledge of the good'. If this were the case this valuable aspect also of 'being educated' would be dependent upon a knowledge condition, though the knowledge would be of a different type from that involved in depth and breadth of understanding. Socrates and Plato, it might be argued, provided the clue to this sort of knowledge in their thinking about the arts; for they connected knowledge in this sphere with sensitization to standards intrinsic to a pursuit or a project. As Socrates pointed out, in his answer to Thrasymachus, anyone who is skilled in anything has regard for the standards which are constitutive of excellence in his art. He does not just know *about* them; he also cares about them and is committed to them. This notion of sensitization to standards, which are connected with the point of the activity, provides a common element in both theoretical and practical pursuits. For to engage in a theoretical pursuit is not just to engage in idle or sporadic curiosity; it is rather to have regard to standards of clarity, relevance, consistency, and correctness which are intimately connected

with the pursuit of truth. Practical pursuits involve such standards as well, in so far as they are transformed by theoretical
understanding; but they also involve additional standards
derivative from the practical purposes which they embody.
Being educated, therefore, involves a capacity for absorption
and enjoyment which is connected with sensitization to
standards which structure activities and pursuits.

If the Socratic conception of 'knowledge of the good'
provides the key to the analysis of the non-instrumental aspect of 'being educated', then knowledge enters into the concept of being an educated person in three ways: viz. depth of
knowledge or theoretical understanding, breadth of knowledge
involved in all-round development and in 'cognitive perspective', and 'knowledge of the good'. The value condition of
'being educated' would therefore be dependent upon various
aspects of knowledge conditions. The question might then be
asked, however, whether the kind of non-instrumental attitude involved in 'knowledge of the good' bestows value on a
state of mind irrespective of the pursuit in which it is exercised. A golfer might exhibit such an attitude, but would this
bestow value on his state irrespective of the value of golf as
an activity? Or, does the value of golf and other activities
depend upon the opportunities which its standards provide
for skill, precision, foresight, resourcefulness, and so on? And
what about the problem posed by anti-social activities such as
burglary. Do we jib at the suggestion that burglary might be
one of the pursuits of an educated person because, as a matter of contingent fact, most people do it for gain rather than
for love? Or do we rule it out simply because its anti-social
character shows lack of all-round development?

Questions like these are pertinent not just to the analysis
of 'being educated' but to ethical theory generally. They are
similar to problems presented by cases of e.g. autonomous or
conscientious men who display these qualities of mind in
activities that seem trivial or anti-social. Additional value, of
course, accrues to activities in so far as they fall under interpersonal moral principles such as justice, benevolence, and
freedom, or in so far as they involve the value of truth. The
question is only about the possibility of there being a distinct
source of value which can be attached to qualities of mind,

15

which can be exhibited in a vast range of activities which may or may not fall under such other principles, e.g. games. This is an issue of considerable importance in the context of educating a whole nation; for there are many who are not likely to go far with theoretical enquiries and who are unlikely to develop much depth or breadth of understanding to underpin and transform their dealings as workers, husbands, and fathers. But there are many challenging and skilful activities in which they can delight, irrespective of the money or fame which they might bring. And not all such activities are of manifest social importance.

Such problems posed by the concept of 'being educated' were, of course, immanent in the previous analysis of the concept of 'education'. But the breaking of the connexion, which I assumed, between 'education' and the development of an 'educated man', has helped to focus attention on them, especially in relation to the importance of the different ways in which knowledge enters into this analysis. The breaking of this connexion has also helped to explain uneasiness which I have always felt about previous ways of answering objections to the old analysis which presupposed this connexion. For instance, as can be seen from 2 (ii) above, there is the difficulty presented by the fact that we talk quite naturally about Spartan education. Now it would be almost a contradiction to speak of an educated Spartan; for 'educated', as qualifying a person, keeps its association with 'an educated man', and one of the things which we know about most of the Spartans is that they were not educated men. Nevertheless they did have various methods of rigorously disciplining and training their children. 'Spartan education', therefore, sounds quite all right because we are relying on the original more generalized concept. Similarly 'specialized education' can be dealt with more simply than by suggesting a parallel with 'intuitive knowledge'. For it has always been customary, in the generalized use of 'education', to particularize the area in which training or instruction was concentrated. So there would be nothing inappropriate in talking either about special education or general education. There does seem to be a difference, too, between asking whether a person has been educated and whether he is an educated man; for the former could be taken as meaning just 'Has he been to school?', whereas the latter suggests much more than this.

Making a distinction between these two concepts of 'education' also enables me to deal with the dissatisfaction felt about certain things that I have said about aims of education. Processes of education, I have argued, are those that lead up to the development of an educated person; so statements about *the* aim of education must be tautological or function as persuasive definitions. For if we say something very general such as that the aim of education is the development of desirable states of mind in people this is like saying that the aim of reform is to make men better. Similarly if it is said that *the* aim of education is to initiate people into what is worth while with some depth and breadth of understanding, it is almost tautological. If something more specific is put in, such as to make men God-fearing citizens, then the statement of the aim is beginning to function as a persuasive definition. Statements about x's aim, or about *an* aim, on the other hand, specify more precisely the particular qualities that are taken to be the attributes of an educated man — e.g. critical thinking, integrity of character, etc. So any statement about an aim, or about x's aim of education, emphasizes features of a person that are part of the understanding of what it means for him to be 'educated'. Of anything that we can call an aim of education we can also say 'So that's what you take an educated person to be like'. This analysis is corroborated by the fact that we do not speak of educating people for, in, or as anything specific; when we want to specify occupational goals which may or may not be compatible with educating people, we speak of training them — e.g. for business, in carpentry, as dentists. Sometimes it is said that we educate people for life. But this vacuous kind of completion can be interpreted as a way of trying to fit the generality suggested by 'educated' into an instrumental type of mould.

These conceptual points about aims of education are pertinent if we are thinking about processes of education as those that are involved in the development of an educated person. If, on the other hand, we are relying on the more general notion of 'education' as one that indiscriminately marks out a vast range of practices concerned with bringing up, rearing,

17

instructing, etc., we might think instrumentally of education
— i.e. we might not connect it with purposes that are part of
our concept of an educated person. We might talk of 'driver
education' or of education being a good investment because
it increases productivity. I do not think that we would say
that we were educating someone for business or to be a den-
tist, because we would be looking at the process from the
inside, and when we take up this stance the associations of
trying to produce an educated person take over. But we
might say, more from the outside, that an aim of education is
to get a better job. In other words I do not think that we
tend to use 'educate' as a task verb without thinking of the
various achievements connected with being an educated man.
But we do use it descriptively, from the outside, in a way
which links what is going on with goals which are extrinsic
to our concept of an educated person. Talking about an 'educational' process suggests much less than talking about an
'educative' one.

In brief the distinction between 'education' as used by
those who think of what is going on as leading up to the
emergence of an educated person and between 'education' as
a word still used, as it was once entirely used, to refer to a
vast range of practices concerned with bringing up children, is
an important one. Making this distinction helps to clarify the
ways in which we use the term 'education' and takes care of
most of the problems that arise if all uses are analysed with
the model in mind of 'education' being a term like 'reform'.
It also preserves whatever was of value in the previous analysis.

6   The limitation and point of analysis

It might be asked what the point is of attempting to sort out
these two concepts of 'education', especially when the more
specific concept of 'education' retains much of its old inde-
terminacy. There is point, I think, because there are these
two concepts in current use and, if one believes in the values
associated with the second, more specific concept, any
attempt to make these values more explicit not only aids
clarity, which is a cardinal intellectual virtue, but also may do

something to shift people's attention towards giving due weight to them. It does not seem to me that, at this particular juncture of history, there is much danger of people losing sight of the mundane, instrumentally oriented operations which the term 'education' has traditionally covered. On the contrary my impression is that people are only too prone to view education in an instrumental way. Education is very much in the public eye, but, from my point of view, for very limited reasons. I suppose that governments see it mainly as the source of trained manpower and that the average man sees it as the vehicle of social mobility. There is also a growing tendency to use the word 'education' to up-grade mundane activities by trading on the values associated with being an educated man. Driving instruction, for instance, becomes 'driver-education' without any radical transformation of the nature of the courses provided. To draw attention, therefore, to the connexion between 'education' and the ideal outcome of an 'educated man', and to maintain that we ought to use words like 'training' or 'instruction' when we do not connect what we are doing with such an ideal, is an aid to communication in the service of an over-all ideal.

But, to paraphrase Wittgenstein, conceptual analysis leaves everything as it is. For the question remains whether it is desirable to lay stress on knowledge and understanding in this way, to be concerned about all round development and intrinsic motivation. To deal with issues of this sort we have to go into ethics and social philosophy as well as into an empirical analysis of the contemporary situation. Conceptual analysis can of itself contribute little to answering such questions, but it can pose them in a more precise form. The issues arising from this analysis are predominantly ethical, but arise in a specific enough manner to avoid many of the most boring and unprofitable aspects of recent ethical discussion — e.g. about whether ethical discourse must be 'prescriptive', and about whether there are any formal ways of delimiting the domain of 'the moral'. We are taken straight into the heart of live ethical discussion, which is concerned with the *content* of what is valuable. The following types of question are posed:

(a) In the realm of 'the good' what makes pursuits so

19

worthwhile that children should be initiated into them? Is their worthwhileness a function of the manner in which they can be pursued (e.g. with love, with regard to the standards immanent in them, with intelligence, resourcefulness, courage, etc.) or are there other grounds for saying that some pursuits are more worthwhile than others, excluding their relationship to interpersonal principles?

(b) What sort of justification can be given for the pursuit and possession of knowledge and understanding? Is it a different type of justification than that given for the pursuit of other worthwhile activities? Is, for instance, some form of transcendental justification possible for the pursuit of knowledge in addition to the types of justification dealt with under (a)? What value can be assigned to breadth as distinct from depth of knowledge? What status is to be ascribed to the sort of knowledge which Socrates referred to as 'knowledge of the good'?

(c) If knowledge is thought to enhance the value of practical pursuits does the 'enhancement' derive from the sort of value dealt with in (a)? Or does it derive from some source independent of (a) dealt with in (b) which is concerned with the peculiar status of truth as a value?

(d) What relationship do values dealt with in (a) have to human excellences such as autonomy, integrity, courage, etc.?

(e) What relationship do values of type (a) and (d) have to interpersonal principles such as justice and the consideration of interests?

Hare once claimed that, if moral philosophers addressed themselves to the question 'How shall I bring up my children?', many of the dark corners in ethics might thereby be illuminated. (Hare, 1952, pp. 74—5.) He was thinking more of the realm of interpersonal principles than of that of 'the good'; but the question is equally pertinent in both realms. My claim is that this fresh attempt at the analysis of the concept of 'education' does something to present in a more specific way the tasks that lie ahead which are of central importance not just for the philosophy of education but for ethical theory in general.

Notes

1 My thanks are due to the Australian National University for the facilities provided for me as a Visiting Fellow which enabled me to write this paper and to Geoffrey Mortimore of the Philosphy Department at the ANU for his constructive comments on a first draft of it.
2 I owe this suggestion to Mrs Nancy Glock who first put it to me in a very persuasive way in a seminar at the Harvard Graduate School of Education in March 1968.

References

Hare, R. M. (1952) *The Language of Morals* (Oxford University Press).
Peters, R. S. (1966) *Ethics and Education* (Allen & Unwin, London).

2   The meaning of quality in education

Introduction

Confronted with the various manifestations of the 'escalation' of education, those who work in educational institutions often maintain that such escalation is bound to be at the expense of the 'quality' of education. More must mean worse. Similarly teachers often maintain that introducing a 'comprehensive' principle, which will alter the distribution of secondary education, must lead to a diminution of quality.

There is, no doubt, much truth in these protestations, just as there is, no doubt, much truth in the claim that Englishmen are now more 'free' than they were in the Middle Ages. The trouble is that there is too much truth in them. By this I mean that such claims are capable of so many different interpretations that massive assent to them conceals a multitude of different interpretations of what is meant. Hard-headed economists therefore get impatient because of the woolliness of educators. This is largely because such claims mean too little because they mean too much.

There is an additional source of confusion if the term 'quality' is used instead of a more general term of appraisal such as 'good'. It encourages educators or economists to think that questions of comparability can be answered by calculation. If one asks whether, educationally speaking, a school for a selected academic élite is better than one for all levels of ability, the obvious reply is that the answer will depend on the respects in which they are compared. For 'good' always goes along with variable criteria of application. If, on the other hand, one asks whether one school or educational system is of higher quality than another, the suggestion is that some kind of straightforward comparison is possible. As this is almost never the case with questions of comparability in education, the use of the word 'quality' gives rise to inappropriate expectations. In actual fact multiple criteria are almost always involved in educational decisions. In so far, therefore, as the term 'quality' suggests that there is some one respect in which things are being compared it is an unfortunate term to use in most educational contexts.

I propose to elaborate this thesis as follows:

Section I. I say something about the concept of 'quality'.

Section II. I show that there must necessarily be multiple criteria involved in talking about quality in education.

Section III. I distinguish criteria other than educational ones by reference to which what goes on in schools and colleges is assessed. The first group of these is what I call 'extrinsic objectives' of educational institutions.

Section IV. The second group of these is what I call 'social principles' involved in the organization and distribution of education.

Section V. I draw out the implications of this analysis for educational decisions.

The concept of 'quality'

The term *qualitas* was a translation of the Greek ποιότης which was used by Plato and Aristotle to pick out what was distinctive of a thing, its essence. A thing's qualities were the attributes which distinguished it from other types of things. (Compare the primary and secondary qualities of things in Galileo, Descartes, Locke.) It was also used more generally to pick out attributes of people, qualities of mind and character, such as independence and honesty — usually good qualities.

A more general use then developed with which we are now familiar. We speak of *the* quality of a thing, quality *in* something, a thing *of* quality, a thing's quality, as distinct from *a* quality of a thing or a thing's qualities. These are normative expressions for intimating excellence or pre-eminence in respect of some quality or qualities in the first more descriptive sense.

It is not the case, however, that things can have quality, generally speaking, in respect of any of their characteristics. If we speak of a horse of quality, or of the quality of a knife, we would not have in mind their colours, though colour would

23

be one of their characteristics. Quality in the normative sense relates to pre-eminence in characteristics that are taken to be *distinctive* of the thing in question. Quality in a horse relates to its proportions or to its capacity for running or jumping; quality in a knife relates usually to its capacity for cutting. Some attributes or qualities in the first descriptive sense are singled out for being the basis for quality in the normative sense, because they are thought to be *important* attributes of the thing in question. But what is the rationale for assigning importance to some attributes rather than others?

On the old Aristotelian view the answer to this question was straightforward. Things belonged to natural kinds, and the qualities comprising their essence were, as it were, also ideal features of things of that sort. As is well known, the doctrine of essence conflated definitional properties of a descriptive sort with ideal standards of a normative sort. Rationality was the essence of man though many men exhibited it haltingly. Thus, if Aristotle had been asked for the hallmark of a man of quality, he would have picked out rationality. Historically speaking, however, the norms giving application to the notion of 'a man of quality' were connected with noble birth. Though Aristotle himself thought that good birth, as well as good looks, were an aid to the development of the essence of a man (his rationality), he also thought that such development could take place without them! The norms associated with 'quality' became dissociated from the defining properties of a thing, or its essence. Whatever, therefore, philosophically speaking, is to be made of the doctrine of essential attributes, it is clear that the general normative notion of 'quality' in a thing has become dissociated from any careful attempt to delineate its defining properties. It has become associated with properties which are thought important or valuable — with what is 'essential' to a thing in a normative rather than in a strictly logical sense.

'Quality' in a normative sense, then, is grounded on a quality or qualities of a thing in a descriptive sense, which are thought to be important or valuable. This value derives from either intrinsic or extrinsic considerations. Quality in a painting, for instance, is derivative from intrinsic qualities which it possesses as a work of art. Quality in a knife, on the other hand, derives from qualities such as sharpness and hardness which are valued because of their instrumentality to human purposes. Assessments of quality will therefore depend on: (a) the isolation of distinctive attributes which are thought to be either intrinsically or instrumentally valuable, (b) judgments about whether a particular thing possesses these attributes in a pre-eminent degree. In other words, to talk concretely about 'quality', as distinct from praising something in an undiscriminating way, must always involve making explicit the valued quality or qualities which are presupposed in general judgments about quality.

This over-simplified analysis is sufficient to indicate the difficulties connected with assessing 'quality in education'. There is, to start with, the ambiguity lurking in the frame of reference in which education is viewed. Teachers and others engaged actively in education look at what is going on in terms of its *educational* value. Their valuations, on which their estimates of 'quality' are based, will relate therefore to intrinsic considerations of two types — the first to do with the approximation of their products to their concept of an educated man, and the second to do with the efficacy of various processes of education in achieving approximations to such products out of children who come to them at very different levels of development. 'Quality' for them will therefore be understood partly in terms of level of achievement in relation to some ideal standards, and partly in terms of efficiency relative to the standard of intake. They are concerned primarily with 'quality' which is intrinsic to education. This is to be contrasted with an extrinsic valuation. Politicians and economists, for instance, may envisage different objectives for schools and an educational system generally. They may tend to look on a school in a much more instrumental way, because they may be primarily interested in ensuring the right amount of relevantly trained manpower. 'Quality' for them will therefore depend on valuations which ascribe importance to different qualities in a school or educational system. The complications involved in the concept of education itself, and in the different frames of reference in which it can be viewed, must now be set out in more detail. I will deal first with the quality which is intrinsic to education and will then pass to quality in the extrinsic sense.

Quality intrinsic to education

In any society, some states of mind, and modes of conduct, structured by forms of thought and awareness, are regarded as intrinsically valuable; that is, they are thought to be valuable for what they are rather than for what they lead up to. Sociologists make a similar type of distinction when they speak of the expressive as opposed to the instrumental culture of a community. That some things must be looked upon in this way is obvious enough; for how else could the notion of 'instrumentality' have application? This does not mean, of course, that activities (for example, weaving, cooking, scientific research) cannot be regarded in different contexts as both instrumentally and intrinsically valuable. The question, too, is left open whether such values are relative to a particular society and whether a rational justification can be given for their pursuit. For the purpose of this enquiry it is sufficient merely to indicate the importance of such values as constitutive of a community's way of life: it is not necessary to raise questions about their ethical status.

'Education' is a term which we use for a family of procedures by means of which individuals are initiated into such forms of thought and awareness and into activities and modes of conduct informed by them. We call a person 'educated' who has been successfully initiated, though, of course, this is a matter of degree and there is no resting-place of being completely educated at which anyone could arrive. It is possible for a lot of education to take place by people 'picking things up' when they are not in an explicit learning situation and when no one is setting out to teach them anything. But a great part of education takes place in more explicit contexts in institutions devoted to it, where learning situations are intentionally contrived. It is with education in this latter sense that we are here concerned.

Obviously enough, the over-all 'aim' of education is the development of educated men and women. Determinateness to the notion of 'quality' in education, therefore, can only be given by getting clearer about the criteria built into the notion of *being educated*. But 'quality' in education could also be taken to describe the efficacy of the *procedures of initiation* in the development of such educated men and women. There could, therefore, be:

1 *Product* judgments of quality, which related purely to the degree to which those who had been at a school or a college satisfied the multiple criteria involved in 'being educated'.

2 *Process* judgments of quality, which took careful account of the state of students before they entered such institutions and measured the extent to which they had progressed towards being educated from a given base-line.

To give an example: if 'quality' was thought of only in the *product* sense, then a school with a highly selective intake, which turned out a high proportion of students who reached university entrance standard, would exhibit it in a pre-eminent degree. If, however, it was thought of in the process sense, a school in a slum area, where the delinquency and illiteracy rate was high, would exhibit it if a fair proportion of its pupils obtained some kind of recognized school-leaving certificate, and if none of them was brought up before the juvenile court. The notion of 'quality' in the process sense could not, of course, be applied without the notion of 'quality' in the product sense; for the efficacy of processes of education could not be estimated unless we had an idea of their ideal outcome in the form of an 'educated man'.

What then is an educated man? What criteria are built into this from which notions of quality in the product sense derive?

What, second, can be said about the characteristics of institutions, curricula, teachers, and procedures which encourage the development of quality in the product sense and hence give content to the notion of quality in the process sense?

These questions provide a framework for the discussion of 'quality' in education.

Product criteria of being 'educated'

There is no one quality of mind characteristic of an educated

27

man. Indeed it is because multiple criteria are necessary to explicate what is meant by being educated that discussions about the aims of education are so common, for attempts to formulate aims of education are attempts to emphasize or concentrate attention on criteria built into the concept of being educated. They are attempts to give specific content to the notion of an educated man.

It is, however, possible to produce a formal framework of criteria which can help to systematize such statements of aims, under three main headings:[1]

1 Commitment to what is regarded as valuable in itself   To be educated suggests having developed, to a certain extent, a 'non-instrumental' attitude, to be disposed to engage in things, e.g., science, weaving, cookery, for what there is in them as distinct from what they may lead on to or bring about. Crucial in this is the development of an autonomous attitude towards learning, together with concentration, perseverance, absorption, and a general attitude of spontaneous enjoyment.

In terms of this criterion no special priority is given to purely theoretical pursuits, though traditionally these have been picked out as those which have supreme value in themselves. There is no reason, however, why a practical activity such as engineering should not be pursued with a similar delight in its intrinsic values. Bridges can be built by engineers who take a delight in constructing an object of enduring worth; it is not only poems, mathematical theorems, and scientific theories that are the product of men with this sort of attitude. The fact that practical activities are more often undertaken purely to satisfy some extrinsic need should not lead us to think that they must always be undertaken with this instrumental attitude. After all, poems can be written on request, for example, to celebrate a victory, and many scientific discoveries have been responses to practical pressures. It is true that practical activities have additional value if they are *also* based on theoretical understanding rather than being mere exhibitions of know-how or knack. But that brings us to the next criterion.

2 *Knowledge and understanding (together with the appro-priate affect)* Being educated implies more than being just skilled, even if the skill is exhibited in some worthwhile pursuit such as music, ballet, or engineering. It involves 'knowing that', not just 'knowing how'. This requires, in the early stages, the development of a basic structure of concepts and categories for distinguishing characteristics of the world from the product of wishes, fears, and imaginings. The basic skills of reading and writing have then to be acquired so that the range and articulateness of experience can be extended and its expression better controlled and communicated. Differentiated modes of awareness must then be developed — scientific, mathematical, moral, interpersonal, historical, aesthetic, religious, philosophical. This must be done in a way which involves not an inert understanding, but a concern for the values underlying them, for example, respect for truth and for persons, sensitivity to suffering and to 'significant form' (see criterion 1).

Within these forms of awareness the distinction has to be made between: (a) knowing facts and mastering a body of knowledge; (b) understanding principles and theories which provide backing to (a), and being able to interpret experience in the light of them; (c) familiarity with, and a degree of mastery of, the procedures by means of which (a) and (b) have been acquired and can be assessed, criticized and developed (e.g., scientific method in the case of science). This permits some kind of autonomous problem-solving, exploration, or evaluation in the relevant form of awareness.

To be educated a person must at least have got as far as (b) and have some familiarity with (c) even if he lacks the mastery of such procedures.

'Quality' in education based on this criterion would relate both to the level of discrimination and understanding achieved and to a multitude of virtues exhibited in these forms of awareness. Some virtues would be those very general moral virtues which are necessary preconditions for the pursuit of truth in any form, for example, respect for facts, for the givenness of materials, and for people as sources of argument, willingness to change one's opinions in the face of facts and arguments, impartiality, humility, tolerance. There are also other general virtues of a more 'intellectual' sort — consistency, originality, accuracy, clarity, precision, sense of relevance, imagination. These would be the most general criteria of 'quality' shared by all forms of awareness. There would then be others which are more specific to the distinct forms of awareness, for example, objectivity and keenness of observation in science, clarity and rigour in mathematics.

3 'Wholeness' There are many nowadays who advocate a curriculum consisting of fields of study (for example, classics, politics, education, geography, the European mind, the seventeenth century) rather than the separate study of 'pure' forms of thought. They argue both that the interest of pupils is thereby better aroused and sustained and that the compartmentalized mind of the specialist is thereby avoided. Whatever the facts are about such claims (and who has conducted the investigations necessary to pronounce on the matter?) the educator's demand for such 'wholeness' is understandable; for being 'educated' rules out being narrowly confined to one form of awareness just as it rules out gearing knowledge entirely to extrinsic ends (criterion 1). 'Education is of the whole man', that cliché so often enunciated from public platforms, is therefore a conceptual truth in that we would not call a person who is narrowly specialized an educated man. This does not mean, of course, that an educated man must not be trained in something. It only rules out the possibility of his being *just* trained. A trained artist, scientist, or historian is not necessarily an educated man, for he may have a deep but circumscribed understanding confined to one of these spheres. To what extent a person has to develop in all the various forms of awareness in order to be educated would be difficult to determine. The main function of this criterion is to rule out narrow specialism rather than to suggest positive requirements. Quality in education can therefore relate in some way to such a criterion of 'all-round understanding'.

This, then, is a framework for classifying different criteria of 'quality' in education, in so far as this relates to 'aims of education', i.e., to our concept of an educated person. Obviously enough, some aspects of 'quality' will be more relevant than others at different stages of development, and the predominant 'aims' of primary, secondary, and higher education can be related to these emphases. Up to about the age of 6, the emphasis will be on the development of cognitive-affective structure and its accompanying virtues, e.g., accuracy (see criterion 2) together with the development and disciplining of curiosity, constructiveness, sympathy, and other motivations which are vital as underpinning the different forms of awareness (see criterion 1). After the acquisition of basic skills (at about the age of 8), a start can be made with building up bodies of knowledge in a way that encourages both precision and an inquiring attitude. When the child passes from the stage of concrete operational thought (at about the age of 12+), the development of a more abstract understanding (see criterion 2) can proceed and lead gradually into the understanding and mastery of procedures (see criterion 2(c)) in at least some form of awareness. This must be done in a way that does not produce narrow specialism (see criterion 3). 'Quality' in higher education will therefore involve a very different emphasis from 'quality' in primary education. But the emphasis at each stage must be related to the general concept of an educated man which has been outlined.

If educational administrators were concerned with comparability questions about the promotion of education on purely educational grounds, the existence of so many qualities falling under (a) *commitment to intrinsic values*, (b) *knowledge and understanding*, and (c) *'wholeness'*, in virtue of which 'quality' could be assigned to the end-products, would itself constitute a major headache. Of course in these terms, if there were no schools above the secondary level in one system, and many institutions of higher education in another, it might be reasonably said that the latter promoted education of higher quality. Similarly, if teaching resources were so thinly spread that few people advanced much further than the acquisition of basic skills, it might well be said that education had almost no quality at all. But how could there be comparison even in purely educational terms between three schools, one of which turned out deeply committed but rather ignorant people, with a modicum of all-round

31

understanding, another which turned out deeply committed specialists in, for example, science or classics, but with little general knowledge, and another which turned out well disciplined specialists with some kind of all-round understanding but with little commitment to continue learning and discovery after they left school? And on what grounds could a school concentrating on classical studies be deemed to provide education of higher quality than one concentrating on science and mathematics? Obviously if a school provided education satisfying all three main criteria it would be of higher quality than the one satisfying only one or two criteria. But how could comparability questions be settled involving judgments between the different criteria? Similarly, there are probably grounds for saying that poetry is qualitatively superior to push-pin. But how could its quality be compared with that of logic?

But this is only the beginning of the headaches, even when schools and educational systems are looked at in terms of purely educational criteria. For there is also the problem introduced by the distinction between 'quality' considered absolutely in the product sense and relatively in the process sense. To this we must now turn.

Process criteria of educational procedures

As explained above, 'quality' in education can be looked at absolutely as defined by reference to criteria 1 — commitment to intrinsic value, 2 — knowledge and understanding, and 3 — 'wholeness', or it can be regarded more relatively in terms of the degree of development along these lines from the base-line of the intake of an institution. Educators are more likely to be interested in 'quality' in the latter sense. So, in tackling questions to do with the efficiency of different educational procedures, the first thing to do would be to test the attainment level of the intake in relation to criteria 1, 2, and 3. If it were then found that more distance towards the ideal of an educated person was covered by one school rather than another, relative to the base-line from which they both started, it would be reasonable to say that the former had more quality in respect of its educational procedures, though it would be very difficult to determine the extent to which this depended on the academic qualifications of the staff or on their personalities, on the teaching methods employed, on the types of incentive or punishment current in the school, on the type of social control used, or on the sheerly physical conditions and equipment.

Assuming, however, that such a comparison of quality between schools were possible, which was based on its pre-eminence in respect of its educational procedures, how could the quality of education in a school with very efficient educational *procedures* be compared with that of a school with less efficient procedures, whose *products* progressed much further towards the ideal of being educated though starting from a base-line well in advance of that of the school with more efficient educational procedures?

This illustrates once again the impossibility of comparisons in terms of 'quality' when the approved qualities which form the basis for estimates of quality are not homogeneous. It has been argued that, as education necessarily involves multiple criteria, such comparisons in terms of quality are seldom possible. We can say that education has quality if it exhibits some of the criteria associated with 'education', in either the product sense or in the process sense, to a pre-eminent degree. But it is usually very difficult to say that there is more or less quality, because of the multiplicity of the criteria involved.

These criteria do, however, enable us to pass judgments on schools and systems if their products satisfy *none* of the criteria previously outlined. The Spartan system, for instance, is more aptly described as a system of training than as a system of education. Certainly it turned out men who were skilled in war and steeped in the military virtues. The Spartans were also, at their best, dedicated to the cause of Sparta and to a particular way of life which has become proverbial. But we would not call them *educated* men, and hence would hesitate to speak of their educational system, because they lacked two of the most important properties of being educated.

First, as the Athenians were only too ready to point out, they had no understanding of the principles underlying their

33

form of behaviour. They managed well in Sparta or in well-defined military situations outside. But when they attempted to govern a colony they were hopeless. Their failure to grasp 'the reason why' of things made them ready victims of politicians, priests, and profligates. Second, they were very *narrowly* trained. They lacked aesthetic awareness, inter-personal sensitivity, historical understanding, and much else besides. It would be mere stipulation to lay down in the case of a people like the Athenians that their much lauded 'happy versability', or all-round understanding and competence, was of *more* educational value than specialism, or development in depth, which was advocated by Plato and Isocrates, the ad-herents of 'professionalism'. But when we consider a people like the Spartans, who had neither breadth nor depth of understanding, it would, I think, be quite appropriate to say simply that they were not educated. This sort of judg-ment is possible.

The same sort of judgment could be made about children at the early primary stage, or about adults in an undeveloped country where there was only training in the basic skills of literacy and numeracy and a system of training for essential occupations. In cases such as the latter, talk of an 'educa-tional system' is rather like talk about the 'language' of birds. Concepts are attenuated to apply to situations where most, but not all, of the conditions for their application are absent. The concept of 'education' only properly has application when a society has reached a certain level of development, when some theoretical basis to its stock of knowledge has been developed, and when the different forms of awareness have begun to be differentiated.

The concept of 'education' here articulated, because of the very formal nature of the criteria made explicit, is to a large extent culture-free. Its content may vary from civilization to civilization, but the general criteria of a non-instrumental attitude to worthwhile activities, which are pursued with some depth and breadth of understanding, are applicable very widely. The fact that there are many societies to which the concept is not applicable and within which the distinction between being merely trained and being educated is not made, is neither here nor there from the point of view of the validity of the analysis. To take a parallel: at a certain stage, morality as a distinct type of code began to be differentiated from custom and law in the same sort of way as science began to be differentiated from mythology and metaphysics. The fact that in some societies this differentiation has not taken place, and that they have not themselves developed concepts for making these distinctions, does not affect the importance of the distinctions once they have emerged. And just as the concept of the scientist is, in important respects, not confined to any particular society once science has taken root in a number of societies, so also the concept of an educated man may well have developed a similar type of autonomy.

Extrinsic objectives for educational institutions

So far questions of quality in education have been approached from the point of view of the educator who is concerned with the promotion of *education*. There are others, however, such as economists and politicians, who regard such a preoccupation as somewhat precious. What is the good, they argue, of schools turning out highly educated people who are specialists in classics or in literature, when the country needs engineers and statisticians? What is the good even of technological institutions spending vast resources on turning out technologists when the same amount of money could be used to produce many more skilled technicians who are urgently needed by the country in greater quantities than technologists? It might, of course, be argued that experience has shown that, in government and industry, highly educated personnel are in fact of more use in the long run than those who are narrowly trained; but such an argument for 'quality' in education would still derive from objectives which are extrinsic to education. Similarly, it can reasonably be argued that technical training can be conducted in such a way that a person emerges who is educated as well. Devoted and sensitive engineers can be much more educated men than scholarly pedants. But this is not now the point at issue.

What is at issue here is the different frame of reference within which what goes on in schools and colleges is now being viewed, which will determine the type of quality

35

assigned to it. From this new point of view of social fitness the Spartans could be said to have had a system of training that was admirably suited — for a certain period — to their national needs. This was quite compatible with their having almost no *educational* system at all. In so far as the Spartan system could be said to have had 'quality', the criteria in terms of which this was estimated would be quite different. It would relate to the social relevance of their training and to the efficiency with which it was conducted in relation to this type of objective.

It was pointed out in section I that qualities of something could be singled out as the basis for quality because of either their intrinsic or their instrumental value. In section II we were concerned only with values intrinsic to education in the sense that we only considered quality deriving from: (a) *product* criteria of being educated, and (b) *process* criteria of efficiency relating purely to the development of education.

We are now passing to a consideration of quality based on instrumental value. Though there is an inappropriateness (on which I will not now expatiate, as it is not germane to my argument) in education itself being assigned value on instrumental grounds, it is obviously the case that what goes on in schools can be viewed in this instrumental way. Just as the Spartans were not concerned with the refinement, sensitivity, and depth of understanding of their young men but only with their courage, obedience, and ability to fight, which were qualities required by their form of state, so an economist might think of schools in relation to their ability to provide relevantly trained manpower. He would, therefore, tend to think of quality in terms of efficiency of *training* relative to the type of posts to be filled, and efficiency of selection in routeing the right sort of personnel to these posts. When politicians grumble at universities for not being responsive to social needs, they are looking at what goes on in these institutions from the point of view of these extrinsic objectives. From this point of view, an institution that encourages Egyptology rather than engineering is of poor quality because of its lack of instrumental value.

Arguments could, of course, be mounted for showing why, whatever is done about Egyptology, a lot of money must be spent on engineering, which would be elaborations of the Marxist truism that a man must eat if he is to engage in higher pursuits. Any community must hand on the knowledge and skills necessary to earn a living. Without these, any large-scale provision for education is a pipe-dream. What level of material achievement is necessary for this is difficult to say. There can, however, be too much overplaying of the economist's hand in this sphere — witness ancient Athens and the modern kibbutzim.

In reply to the more banal type of economist it is argued that education matters as well as the pool of trained manpower. I recently heard an impassioned plea on a government committee for the importance of music in the primary school. The complaint was that there was every encouragement to science and French because of their obvious technical and commercial importance, but the claims of music were too often overlooked because of its lack of instrumental value. Such appeals are not based, of course, on comparisons of the 'quality' of music as distinct from that of science or French as part of a person's education. They are demands that what goes on in schools should not be looked at purely in one frame of reference. The 'wholeness' of the educated man, of which an aesthetic sense is an important aspect, must not be overlooked by those who think in terms of industrial efficiency and the export market. They are elaborations of the Socratic saying that it is not mere life that is worth living but the good life. And the good life includes that of the scientist and the engineer. There is nothing inherently 'uneducational' about engineering. It can be indulged in with deep understanding by men who value what there is in it rather than what it leads on to, and who have a vision of much else besides. That, I must repeat, is not the point at issue.

What *is* at issue is the frame of reference within which the 'quality' of what goes on in schools is to be assessed. Engineering and Egyptology can both be looked at from the point of view of their educational value. From this point of view a general comparison would be very difficult to make; it would depend so much on how they were conceived and taught. Presumably Egyptology, like Latin, could be taught

37

in a way which was so dreary that the values intrinsic to it went by the board. Engineering, on the other hand, could be taught by someone like Leonardo. But if the two were to be compared in respect of their instrumental value to a country's economy, there could be little doubt about which had most quality in *this* respect. Thus, though the two might be compared either for their educational value, or for their contribution to the economy, no comparison in terms of quality would be possible if criteria of quality were derived from intrinsic considerations in the case of the one as distinct from extrinsic considerations in the case of the other.

This does not mean, of course, that any decision about which to encourage would be completely arbitrary, even if intrinsic considerations were weighed against instrumental ones. It would depend very much on contingent questions to do with the community's resources and the level of training achieved. Obviously, too, pursuits such as science and mathematics are highly impregnated with *both* types of value. There may be a paradox, too, akin to the old paradox of hedonism, which is that science may actually have more instrumental value if it is not taught too much under this aspect. But the point is that these sorts of decision about priorities, though not arbitrary, are not decisions based on estimates of quality. Quality, as has been repeatedly stressed, must be estimated in respect of some distinctive qualities. If the distinctive qualities are not in the same dimension, comparability questions are unanswerable.

In brief, one can talk about the quality of education which exists in an institution in relation to the different criteria previously outlined; one can also talk about the quality of training or selection in an institution in accordance with the efficiency displayed by the institution in relation to extrinsic objectives set by politicians and economists rather than by educators. One can also talk about the quality of an institution in respect either of its education or in respect of the training and selection which it provides. What one cannot do, however, is compare institutions for quality in general without making clear whether it is their quality as educational or as training institutions which is up for assessment.

Social principles and educational institutions

Such comparability questions are further complicated by another set of criteria which might be regarded as a ground of desirability. In a democratic society, for instance, questions could be asked about the authority structure of the school to see the extent to which authority was rationalized. Is formal provision made for the staff and students to have adequate opportunities for sharing in meaningful and significant decision-making? Within the educational system too, desirability might be claimed in respect of the degree of autonomy that the school itself, and especially its headmaster, possessed in determining matters to do with its own educational objectives. There could then be questions of fairness and freedom. Does the school recognize the importance of different types of pursuit, thereby setting the stamp of approval on a wide variety of avenues of achievement and giving concrete implementation to the demand for equality of consideration? Does the curriculum formally permit many options and allow an area of discretion to its pupils, thereby making some degree of freedom a reality? Without formal provisions of this sort the democratic ideals of 'equality of opportunity' and of 'the self-realization of the individual' are empty shibboleths.

Such moral principles might of course be regarded from the point of view of their educational value as influencing the development of desirable moral attitudes on the part of pupils, which would be one of the obvious forms of understanding characterizing an educated person. A necessary condition, for instance, of a person learning to be fair may be that he is brought up in an institution in which this is prominent as a distributive principle. But such principles can also be regarded as valuable in themselves, in that they are institutional implementations of social principles fundamental to democracy. But the insistence on such principles, relating to the distribution and organization of education, may or may not lead to higher quality of education estimated in terms of purely educational criteria, and they may or may not further extrinsic objectives to do with training and selection. Quite obviously, adherence to such principles sometimes militates against efficiency measured in terms of training and selection e.g. as in a girls' school in which very few girls can be persuaded to take up science. The country may need linguists, chemists, and statisticians, but if most girls steadfastly prefer to 'realize themselves' in music, cookery, and literature, how can their demands be ignored if a country is committed to liberty and equality? Only if (as in Michael Young's book on education and equality)[2] a community were to (a) set its face against education, (b) ignore liberty and equality and respect for persons, and (c) erect 'productivity' as an overriding extrinsic objective and gear everything that goes on in schools and colleges to this, could clear-cut qualitative comparisons be made.

Obviously, too, insistence on principles such as liberty and equality, if they are interpreted in a certain way, may militate against the quality of education in both the product and process senses (see p. 27). It may be argued that a comprehensive system, which enshrines a particular interpretation of the principle of equality, may entail in the long run less quality in the *products*. On the other hand it may be argued that, though fewer pupils achieve a high standard according to criteria involved in the product, the average standard is higher. And how can systems be compared in respect of *quality* if, in one system, say 10 per cent of its pupils achieve a very high standard and the rest a very low standard, whereas, in another system, the standard attained is distributed much more according to the normal curve? It might well be said that the second system was *fairer* or that it permitted more *liberty*. But this is different from saying that one or the other is superior in quality.

The same sort of point might be made in relation to criteria relating to educational procedures. One school might, for instance, concentrate its resources on the improvement of very dull children and leave the rest to fend for themselves, relatively speaking. This might be unfair to the brighter children whose relative improvement was poor compared with that of the duller children. But how could the quality of the educational procedures of such a school be compared with that of another which brought about a mediocre improvement in all its pupils? Such principles of organization and distribution do not introduce, as it were, a criterion of quality in addition to the ones already made explicit; they introduce normative considerations for the making of decisions which are distinct from those which constitute the grounds of quality.

On the other hand there might be occasions when demands for fairness would seem Utopian. Suppose, for instance, that primary education was being introduced into an under-developed society, and suppose that resources were very limited. Whatever differences there may be in emphasis about what constitutes 'quality' in terms of the product at this level, it is known that 'quality' in terms of procedures depends upon a variety of conditions, for example, regular attendance at school, size of classes, length of the school day, knowledge and skill of teachers. If 'education' were too thinly distributed with very limited resources, it would mean that almost nothing of value would be distributed. So it might reasonably be argued that claims deriving from fairness would not be very strong in this sort of case. A similar argument might be put forward for the concentration of resources on the development of one university rather than on the development of several. It might be claimed reasonably that education at this level cannot go on unless there is a concentration of teachers developing different forms of knowledge in one spot. If they are scattered over a number of institutions, with lesser luminaries revolving round them, the quality will be so poor that it is hardly recognizable as university education at all. Insistence, therefore, on expansion because of fairness, or because of the need for certain categories of manpower, might militate against anyone of the required calibre emerging.

Cases like these, where insistence on fairness would be incompatible with the product having any quality, whatever criteria of quality are emphasized, are very different from cases where insistence on equality may mean merely a diminution in quality. To take a parallel: the distribution of a certain type of drug in very small doses might make a minute difference to a multitude of people suffering from a disease; but if it was concentrated on 10 per cent of the cases, they might be cured. Would it be rational to insist on fairness in this sort of case? Many undiscriminating demands for educational expansion, on grounds of fairness or of national need, may be like this. They overlook, too, the multiplier effect of having a few institutions of high quality.

I have illustrated my point about the intrusion of social principles into discussions of quality in education by taking fairness and freedom as particular examples. But the same sorts of point could be made by taking other such social principles. For instance, the diffuse demand in England for 'social integration' in the state schools is obviously at variance with other criteria of quality. But I do not think there is any need for further elaboration of this point.

Implications for administrative decisions

Enough has now been said to illustrate the sorts of complication involved in the attempt to take account of 'quality' in educational decisions. It has been maintained that: (a) If comparative estimates of 'quality' were considered on purely educational grounds, they would be very difficult to make because of the multiple criteria that are necessarily involved in education on the basis of which 'quality' must be assigned; (b) Educational institutions and systems can be looked at in relation to extrinsic objectives to do with social requirements, for example, for relevantly trained manpower. This provides other criteria of 'quality', which may conflict with strictly educational ones; (c) There is a demand that institutions should exemplify the basic social principles of a society in respect of their organization and in respect of the distribution of what is held to be of value. Such social principles provide distinct bases of valuation which may conflict with those which form the bases of 'quality', whether it is intrinsically or instrumentally determined.

The upshot of this analysis is to suggest that when objection is raised to plans for the extension or reorganization of education on the grounds that its 'quality' may suffer, this functions mainly as a warning. It conveys little determinate information. It can be misleading, however, because it may suggest that something rather precise is being said. If it is maintained that the quality of a knife will deteriorate if it is left out in the rain or put on a fire, there can be little misunderstanding about what is meant. For 'quality' is assigned to a knife on the basis of limited and determinate qualities such as hardness and sharpness. But education is so unlike a knife that the suggestion of determinateness conveyed by 'quality' is highly misleading. It would be preferable to say that the education would be worse, which would immediately encourage the appropriate reply, 'In what respects? Do you mean that it would be lacking in depth or in breadth? Or would it lack intrinsic motivations?' These sorts of consideration would then have to be put alongside judgments such as 'socially superfluous', or 'economically irrelevant', or 'less unfair', or 'authoritarian', or 'involving less freedom'. Administrators would then have to make up their minds as to what to do in the light of the facts of the situation, the resources at their disposal, and the pressures put on them, and the importance to be accorded to the variety of valuations involved. This is how things are. Omnibus talk about 'quality' may conceal the complexity of the decisions involved and the fact that there is no straightforward sort of calculation which will enable them to be made.

This is the final point. Educational decisions, like political decisions, necessarily involve not simply moral considerations but judgments about the relative weight to be accorded to considerations falling under different moral principles. Judgments about 'quality' fall under the general principle of the promotion of what is good. There are, however, as has been shown, multiple criteria of 'quality' within this, which necessitate judgment in cases of conflict; for there is no way of calculating the value of dedication to Egyptology as a specialized subject when it is weighed against an all-round education without much depth. Quality, in both these senses, has to be weighed against considerations falling under the more general principle of the promotion of the common good.[3] Drains, roads, and hospitals have to be weighed against pictures and concerts. In an educational context this means that the claims of training and selection for publicly necessary skills have to be weighed against the claims of education in a strict sense. And what sort of a sum is this?

The judgments so far referred to fall within the area of the promotion of what is good, though there are multiple criteria within this area. But, in addition to considerations falling

43

under this principle, there are also considerations falling under the principles of justice, liberty, and respect for persons. I have dealt mainly with those falling under justice for the sake of brevity. But the same sort of points could be made in respect of other principles, which may be mutually antagonistic to each other. The 'independent school' issue in the United Kingdom, for instance, nicely illustrates the clash between fairness, liberty, and the promotion of 'quality' in education.

Leibniz once put into words the Utopian dream of rationalists when he suggested that rational men, confronted with a moral problem, might be able to get round a table with pencil and paper and say to each other, 'Let us calculate'. Bentham tried to implement such a dream with his hedonistic calculus. But, as is well known, he ran up against the problem of qualitative differences in the goods to be promoted. He never produced any good arguments either for the somewhat dubious assumption that the promotion of good is equivalent to the promotion of happiness, or for his contention that the rightness of fairness as a distributive principle depends upon its felicific consequences.

Once the view is abandoned either that there are Platonic seers who have an unclouded vision of what is good and just, or that there is some over-all good such as happiness that can be calculated by experts, political and educational decisions must become a matter of judgment rather than of computation, of weighing up the urgency of claims rather than making purely technical decisions. Presumably, democracy as a form of government is based on the presupposition that there are no moral 'authorities' and that there are vital aspects of political decisions which are matters of judgment, not of computation. With problems of this sort the only rational type of procedure is to arrange for claims and interests to be represented and to work towards some sort of 'solution' by adjustment and discussion.

This is not, of course, to deny that there is a very important place for expertise and computation once its relevance, as falling under one or other of the principles involved, has been shown. The consequences of alternative policies can be roughly predicted, the cost of implementing them can be roughly estimated, and limits can be suggested for what is practicable with given resources. This is obvious enough in a general sort of way. The particular ways in which such expertise is relevant in the educational sphere — especially where questions of 'quality' are at issue — I leave to the appropriate experts who are taking part in this symposium.

Notes

1   This paper was written *before* the author's second thoughts on the concept of 'education' as set out in the first paper. Hence the discrepancies between them — e.g. about Spartan education on p. 36. He is no longer happy even with his second thoughts, and is attempting to work out a further revision. So neither of the 'analyses' of 'education' here presented should be taken as anything more than sighting shots at a highly indeterminate target.
2   Michael Young, *The Rise of the Meritocracy: 1870—2033*, London, Thames & Hudson, 1958.
3   See R. S. Peters, *Ethics and Education,* London, Allen & Unwin, 1966, chapters V and VI.

3 Ambiguities in liberal education and the problem of its content[1]

Introduction

If one was mounting a defence of certain distinctive values in education nowadays I doubt whether one would run up the flag of 'liberal education' in order to mark what one stood for. The term itself suggests the sweetness and light of the nineteenth century rather than the 'relevance' and 'validity' of the twentieth. Liberal policies, too, notoriously lack the positive cutting edge of the radical and the defensive solidarity of the conservative. Nevertheless, in spite of the fact that the term itself is not particularly in vogue, the ideas behind it are; for contemporary complaint is against constraints of any sort, and the unifying idea behind liberal education is that of the unimpeded and unconstrained development of the mind. The concept, therefore, is of considerable contemporary relevance whatever one says about the phrase.

A more fundamental difficulty about the phrase is its endemic ambiguity. It is endemic because, as I have argued before,[2] 'liberal' functions like 'free' in that it suggests the removal of constraints, and there are different types of constraint. There is also the necessity, if clear communication is thought desirable, of stating precisely what it is of value that is being constrained. There are, therefore, bound to be ambiguities inherent in demands for liberal education. In a similar way, when people make demands for 'free schools', further questions must be asked about what they think schools are for and whether it is the curriculum, teaching methods, the organization of the school or external pressures on it, which are constraining.

Common to all interpretations of liberal education, however, is the value placed upon knowledge and understanding. The various constraints are seen as impeding the mind in its quest for it. But it is at this point that ambiguities are most

marked; for there is too little clarity about the type of knowledge that is to be sought. Indeed, as I shall argue, this question has been obscured by the tendency to assimilate the
position of those acquiring knowledge in schools to that of
those advancing knowledge in universities.

1 Three interpretations of liberal education

The ambiguities of what is meant by a liberal education are
embodied in academic folk-lore by the story of the Oxford
scholarship entrant who was asked by a tutor why he wished
to come up to Oxford. 'To benefit from a liberal education,
sir,' he replied. 'And what, pray, is that?' asked the tutor —
'That is what I hope to discover by coming here,' replied the
aspiring scholar. If he had obtained a scholarship and had
studied the classics he would soon have gleaned that the
notion of a liberal education was introduced by the Greeks.
Education was conceived of as a process in which the mind's
development towards knowledge and understanding was not
to be inhibited by being harnessed to vocational or utilitarian ends. Knowledge must be pursued 'for its own sake',
not viewed as instrumental to some other end. This is the
first interpretation of liberal education. It was strongly
supported by nineteenth-century thinkers such as Matthew
Arnold and Cardinal Newman in a context of the rapid
development of technical training and technology. It is still
very influential as a characterization of university education.

The second interpretation of liberal education is a plea
against the mind being confined to one discipline or form of
understanding. Newman's conception of all-round development was, to a large extent, a reaction against the growing
specialization and compartmentalization of knowledge in the
nineteenth century. Nowadays, at any rate at the school level,
liberal education is more or less identified with this demand
for a general education as distinct from a specialized training.
This demand is well exemplified in Paul Hirst's conception of
a liberal education, which involves initiation into all the
distinct forms of knowledge.[3]

A third interpretation of liberal education relates to constrictions on the mind imposed by dogmatic methods of

teaching. An obvious example of this is indoctrination, in which a fixed body of beliefs is implanted in a manner which discourages criticism or an exploration of the grounds on which beliefs are based. Authoritarianism is another example; for the reasoning capacity of the individual is stunted by arbitrariness and by appeals to or demonstrations of the status of the teacher.

These three types of demand do not necessarily coincide. Mary Warnock, for instance, is a passionate advocate of studying things for their own sake, which she sees as one of the hall-marks of quality in education. But she is against general education which she regards as counter-productive in the attempt to achieve quality.[4] Catholic educators, following Newman, often favour the all-round development of the mind; but they are not notorious for condemning authoritarian methods of instruction. Some advocates of progressive methods, on the other hand, such as Dewey, do not espouse the pursuit of knowledge for its own sake; rather they see it as subservient to practical problem-solving. It is, of course, merely competing for an honorific title to ask which of these interpretations of liberal education is the real one.

Having distinguished these three interpretations of 'liberal education' I now propose to examine each in turn in more detail in order to make explicit the positive values in each which are thought to be subject to some kind of constraint, and to ask questions about the type of knowledge which the mind should be free to pursue.

2 Liberal education as knowledge for its own sake

The constraints objected to in the first interpretation are those of utility and vocational relevance. Geometry, for instance, was found to be of great use in the development of plans for irrigation; but it was also studied without such constrictions imposed by practical ends. Indeed, on Plato's view, an understanding of its principles was essential for the mind's development, and hence a crucial element in education. The positive idea underlying this classical conception of liberal education was that man has an essence, which is his rationality, and that the highest form of its exercise is in theoretical pursuits. Education was viewed by him as a process which equips and encourages a man to develop into being fully a man by using his reason to the utmost.

In derivations of this conception of liberal education the 'natural' development of mind is contrasted with the pursuit of knowledge for utilitarian or vocational ends by saying that knowledge is pursued 'for its own sake'. This suggests that the reasons for study are immanent in the study itself as distinct from benefits which might accrue from it. These might be stated in a mundane way by saying that the person did it out of curiosity or out of interest, or in a more Platonic way by saying that the person was led by a passion for grasping principles, for finding the forms in the facts. Alternatively, a more normative note might be struck by mention of the demand to eliminate error and find out what is true. Finally such study might be represented as a form of mastery, as an enjoyable and challenging type of adventure. All such reasons for pursuing knowledge have the common feature that they are intrinsic to the pursuit of it and hence definitive of the mind's untrammelled development. They are to be contrasted with practical ends which are thought to act as constraints or limitations on the mind's development.

In Greek thought this ideal of pursuing knowledge for its own sake was extolled because practical knowledge was thought to involve mingling with the materials of the earth and thus to debase a man's soul, rendering him βαναυσικός. The type of practical knowledge which was displayed in morals and politics was not debasing in the same way, but it lacked the pure unimpeded features of theoretical knowledge and was thus not so valuable. The 'making' which characterized the fine arts was thought to be inferior for rather different reasons connected with the metaphysical status of its products. The net result was that there has been a continuing and influential tradition which has upheld the training of people in theoretical pursuits as the paradigm of liberal education, with a consequent down-grading of the practical. In universities, for instance, the faculties of medicine, engineering and education, are not held in such esteem as the faculties of arts and science. The reasons for this are complex, but one reason is still that they are closely connected with mundane practical problems.

49

It is not my intention in this article to extol the virtues of either theoretical or practical knowledge, still less to discuss the Greek arguments about man's function or essence from which this emphasis on the theoretical stems. Concern with practical ends, however, need not be particularly limiting. Freud's basic concern was to cure his patients, but his speculations about their minds were pretty far-ranging. The solution of educational problems requires excursions into psychology, philosophy and the social sciences in a way which it is very difficult to delimit. Enquiries spring from problems. Some types of practical problems require far-ranging enquiries. Others do not. The same can be said of theoretical problems.

The important difference, I suppose, is that in practical enquiries knowledge is not pursued 'for its own sake'. Interest or curiosity is less likely to draw the medical student to the study of physiology than his consciousness that this type of knowledge is necessary for curing people. It is difficult to see, however, why this makes such enquiries less *valuable* in the absence of a special ethical theory such as the Greek doctrine of function. For practical ends such as the elimination of suffering and the maintenance of security are surely *valuable*. Also the obligatory types of value present in theoretical enquiries, the demand that error must be avoided and virtues such as those of consistency, coherence, and clarity which surround this demand, are present in practical enquiries as well. Indeed they have additional point if practical consequences depend in part upon the truth of the supporting beliefs. Incorrect diagnosis may suggest treatment which leads to the death of a human being. I am not arguing, of course, that the justification of such virtues surrounding the attempt to discover what is true is to be sought in such consequences, only that such consequences give additional point to them. And it is not obvious why this sobering aspect under which such enquiries can be viewed make them any less valuable than if they are conducted purely out of interest or curiosity.

However I must stick to my resolution not to enter into the debate about the value of liberal education and to the task of trying to delimit what is included or excluded by this interpretation of it. This is difficult to decide; for the

50

dichotomy between 'knowledge for its own sake' and 'knowledge for practical ends' is too coarse to throw light on the attitude of the learner towards knowledge. Indeed, as I shall argue later, it is really a distinction developed within the context of the *advancement* of knowledge, which is often transferred to the situation of the learner.

Knowledge for practical ends

The first difficulty is with 'knowledge for practical ends'. For this description conceals a distinction that it is very important to make when considering the motivational structure of learning in institutions such as schools and universities. A typical example would be a boy at school practising on a lathe or a miller because he wanted to be a toolmaker or a medical student learning anatomy because he wanted to cure people. In both cases the knowledge and skill attained is indispensable to the practical activity, and there might be no further end for the sake of which the activity was practised. The boy might just want to make tools; the student might just be very concerned to relieve suffering. They might be oblivious to any thoughts of pay-off in terms of financial reward, approval, status, etc. On the other hand these further ends might exert a strong appeal and infect their learning and general conduct in their practical activities. They might equally well infect the activity of a scientist engaged on pure research; for he might become 'double-minded' in valuing his reputation as much as or more than the pursuit of truth, and be driven by this narcissistic ambition in his studies.

In learning at school these *further* ends are extremely important; for the learning situation is very often geared to obtaining rewards, doing better than others, avoiding punishment, winning status and approval, and passing examinations which are often seen as prerequisites to wealth and status. There are two features of such *further* ends which provide a contrast to the case of the toolmaker interested just in making tools or the medical student with a concern about human suffering. The first is that motives such as greed, envy, fear of disapproval, and ambition, supply ends which exert a variable, extrinsic influence on learning activities. A student

51

may cheat to do better than a rival; he may learn just enough to get by if he wishes to avoid the disapproval of the teacher. His care and effort is not determined by the intrinsic nature of the learning task. By contrast, the medical student with a concern about relieving distress works at tasks which are all determined by their relevance to this end. Ideally he takes care because he cares about the suffering of the patient. In a similar way the toolmaker may be moved by his love of precision, accuracy and neatness which are values instantiated in what he is learning. Thus the motivation to learn is not so dependent on external and variable interpersonal and institutional factors. Second, the knowledge attained in the service of these extrinsic ends is not indispensable to their attainment or in any way constitutive of them. A student can learn geometry to outshine a rival or to please a teacher. But there are other ways of achieving such ends and his knowledge of geometry is not central to the satisfaction obtained. The marks or the smiles are what matter to him, not the knowledge of Euclid. In the other cases, however, the ends cannot be achieved at all without this knowledge or skill. No one can enjoy making tools unless he has mastered a lathe and miller. Also the exercise of the knowledge or skill concerned is central to the satisfaction obtained. For 'ends' like curing a patient or perfecting a tool are unintelligible without reference to the relevant knowledge and skill.

The distinction between 'knowledge for its own sake' and 'knowledge for practical ends' is too coarse to mark these different ways in which practical ends can be pursued. It is also inadequate; for both theoretical and practical activities can be pursued 'for their own sakes' or they can be infected by the pull of all-pervasive motives such as ambition, envy, and greed. Now many argue that the most corrupting influence in life generally, as well as in learning, is the influence of these very motives. As they are very influential in our school system it could be argued that the dichotomy between 'learning for its own sake' and 'learning for practical ends', which is provided by this interpretation of 'liberal education', is a very unhelpful one because it is too coarse to make this crucial distinction. Indeed, because the further ends that go with ambition, greed, envy, etc., can be thought of as 'practical', in contrast to ends provided in theoretical activities by curiosity, concern for truth, etc., it could be argued that the dichotomy is positively misleading. For it tends to confuse the practical with the purely instrumental.

There is also the point that such 'ends' are often represented in too rationalistic a way. Much learning takes place in situations in which there is an implicit expectation of, or association with, something that is desired, but in which the learning is not viewed consciously as a means to attaining it. When children copy their elders or pick up their opinions or attitudes, they are not consciously seeking approval or reward. They may admire the person concerned; there may be warmth in the situation which favours attention; they may be afraid of missing something, or of being out of line. But they are not explicitly learning for the sake of such 'practical ends'.

There are inadequacies, then, in one alternative offered by the dichotomy of 'knowledge for its own sake' and 'knowledge for practical ends' when it is applied to the situation of the learner. For 'knowledge for practical ends' has been shown to gloss over crucial distinctions.

Knowledge for its own sake

But there are also inadequacies in the alternative of 'knowledge for its own sake'. This may rule out various motivations to learn; but what does it rule in? Obviously learning from sheer curiosity or learning because of the interest, novelty, or puzzling features of the subject-matter. But are these the only alternatives to learning for the sake of practical ends?

Suppose a man is exercised about why his friend is rude to him, worried about his own prejudices and uncharitable feelings, or concerned about whether he should be patriotic or feel awe for the sea or at the sight of death. Suppose that he is led by such uneasiness into studies in psychology, ethics, politics, and religion. Is he in such cases pursuing knowledge for its own sake? Notions like 'knowledge for its own sake' and curiosity suggest a stance that is too detached and disinterested to do justice to his concern about such questions. On the other hand, answering them is not obviously connected with any particular course of action or further end to be achieved. For they are applications of the general beliefs and attitudes which are constitutive of his level of understanding and sensitivity as a human being. What is he to make of objects in the natural world and of phenomena such as the dark, thunder, the tides, time, and the changes of the seasons? What is he to make of other people and of their reactions to him and to each other? What is he to think about himself and about questions of ownership? What attitude is he to take towards the cycle of birth, marriage and death? In what way is he to react to authority, suffering, and violence? These are questions arising from the general conditions of human life. Answers to them provide a general framework of beliefs and attitudes within which particular ends are sought and particular puzzles arise. Such practical and theoretical pursuits often bring about a transformation within the general framework. But the framework itself cannot be regarded purely as a deposit left by the pursuit of knowledge for its own sake or for the sake of some practical or extrinsic end.

Advancement of knowledge

These categories are probably very much the reflection of the situation in civilized societies when special institutions are created for the *advancement* of knowledge. Those who advance knowledge in such institutions will either be doing this for its own sake or to prepare people for professions or to contribute to the solution of practical problems in the community. They will, therefore, tend to view the situation of people *acquiring* knowledge when they are being educated as capable of being categorized in the same way as that of those like themselves who are advancing knowledge. They will, therefore, debate about whether students should be encouraged to learn because of the intrinsic interest of the subject, because it will prepare them for a job, or because it will have some other practical use in life. And they will pass on these ways of viewing the acquisition of knowledge to their students from whom teachers are recruited. What will tend to be overlooked is the need to develop beliefs and attitudes which will help a person to make sense of and take up some stance towards the various situations and predicaments that he will inevitably encounter as a human being.

When talking about the educational value of a subject, university teachers such as Mary Warnock[5] stress the enjoyment of working at something for its own sake and the wish to go on with it on one's own. But this, surely, is a delight that can be experienced in a vast range of activities such as cooking, gardening, and carpentry. It is not peculiar to working at subjects such as history or geography. Nor is it possible, as she so rightly points out, for anyone to work in many fields of study in this way which is typical of a person who may go on to discover things for himself. Given, then, that subjects such as these provide all sorts of answers to questions which a man may ask about the world, and human life, how is he to be introduced to this human heritage? Mary Warnock views subjects rather from the point of view of potential research workers; but an equally important educational question is to ask how the products of such work can become significant to the majority of people who are never going to transform such products by their own activity. A person without a consciousness of the historical dimension of current social problems is poorly educated; but does he have to work systematically as a historian to develop such a consciousness? The sort of knowledge that enables a man to understand better the layout of a town in which he is spending a holiday, to appreciate features of the rocks and rivers, or to speculate about the customs of the local inhabitants, is not the product necessarily of any specialized study on his part in history, geography, or anthropology. But it is very much the hall-mark of an educated person. Did he acquire such knowledge for its own sake? Or to accomplish any practical purpose? Parts of it perhaps. But it is just as likely that he picked it up because of his concern to assess the significance of the context in which he has to live his life. Or perhaps he just picked it up from a talkative friend over a pint of beer.

In brief my argument is that there is a body of knowledge, entertained with varying degrees of understanding, that is extremely significant or 'relevant' to a person in so far as it determines his general beliefs, attitudes, and reactions to the general conditions of human life. This is not necessarily acquired for its own sake, as is a field that a person studies in depth out of interest or pure curiosity, or acquired because of its usefulness to particular ends. Liberal education, in the first interpretation, is too often equated with the stance of a scholar pursuing a subject that he loves. There is great value in this type of activity; for it involves not only the joys of mastery and the adventures of discovery, but also intellectual virtues such as clarity, humility, and impartiality of mind. But not all our beliefs are acquired by this sort of activity and many people are not at all drawn to it. They therefore often complain of the irrelevance of learning and are only disposed to apply themselves if they can see the pay-off. Yet if this knowledge and understanding could be presented to them more imaginatively in ways which take much more account of their concerns as human beings, their attitude towards learning might be different.

There is too much of a tendency to regard motivation just as a bundle of interests or needs that the individual brings with him ready made to a learning situation. In truth it is just as much a product of the situation in which he finds himself as something which he brings to it. If an institution is geared towards providing people with levels of qualifications to determine their point of entry to the occupational structure, this is the motivational message which its students will ingest, however hard its teachers work to present learning in a different light. Of course gifted teachers may arouse different attitudes in a few. In others, the desire to pass the required examinations may be reinforced by interests aroused by the subject matter itself once they start to work. But the majority are likely to remain strangers to such non-instrumental attitudes to learning. They learn, if they do, in the way in which the logic of their institutional situation requires them to learn.

State of mind of educated?

There is a question, though, whether people who talk about 'liberal education' in this first interpretation are primarily concerned with the motivation for learning characterizing the 'process' of education. They might be more concerned with the state of mind of the 'product'. A person, for instance, might have learnt mathematics because he saw it as being of practical use, but might gradually have become 'hooked' on it, to use a colloquialism. He might end up by being fascinated by it 'for its own sake'. Alternatively he might have worked at it just because he enjoyed solving these sorts of abstract problems. But later on he might come to appreciate its practical use. Indeed the concern with motivation might be only indirect. When, for instance, Whitehead fulminated against 'inert ideas' he was not directly making a motivational point. He was lamenting the lack of *application* to people's experience of so much that was learnt at school — mere book-learning that did little to transform a person's understanding of situations which he was likely to encounter. He then jumped to the other extreme and argued that knowledge should be 'useful'. Indeed he claimed that education is the art of the 'utilization' of knowledge.[6] But is this really what he meant? Did he not really mean that the knowledge and understanding of an educated person should have *application* in his life, should give him concepts and generalizations for understanding better situations in which he was likely to be placed? Did he mean 'useful' in the strict sense of instrumental to the realization of some practical end?

This dichotomy between 'inert' and 'useful', made in the context of characterizing the type of knowledge that it is important for an educated person to possess, tends to reinforce the dichotomy in motivation between 'for its own sake' and 'for the sake of some practical end'. It encourages the neglect of that same body of knowledge, entertained with varying degrees of understanding, that is extremely significant or 'relevant' to a person in so far as it determines his general beliefs, attitudes, and reactions to the universal conditions of human life. This is neither 'inert' nor 'useful' in any ordinary sense.

I said that Whitehead, in making this distinction, was only indirectly concerned with motivation. By that I mean that he was concerned with knowledge which seems of obvious 'relevance' to a person's situation. Presumably he assumed, like most people, that learning will be improved as well because it will be seen to be relevant by the learner. But this is not necessarily the case, and the same point needs to be made about the kind of knowledge concerned with the human condition which I have assumed to be of some kind of emotional significance to anyone. For even though everyone is likely to be confronted at some time by emotional problems to do with death, personal relationships, authority, violence, etc., these may not seem to be of any particular significance to him while he is at school. That is why, in talking about liberal education, it is important to distinguish the motivational thesis from the sort of thesis developed by Whitehead about the features of the knowledge or understanding that anyone should be encouraged to develop.

My own view is that the content of education should not be determined by what, at any particular moment, the learner finds interesting or important, though obviously this is something of which any good teacher should be mindful. The teacher's task is as much to arouse interest as it is to build on existing interest. The same applies to concern about predicaments like those of death, suffering, and sexual infatuation to which it would be somewhat inappropriate to apply terms such as 'interest' and 'curiosity'. These are likely to compel the attention of students because of the universal emotions which are aroused by such predicaments. But even if they do not immediately do so, something should be done about the development of beliefs and attitudes in this area because of the predictable significance of these predicaments in anyone's life at some time. I am not saying, of course, that the content of education should be centred entirely in this area. Only that it is an important area that tends to be neglected. This neglect is encouraged by the demand that knowledge should be either for its own sake or for its practical use.

3 Liberal education as general education

This sphere of knowledge which seems essential to an educated person, but which proved, in the preceding section, to be very difficult to fit into the categories of acquired 'for its own sake' or 'for the sake of some further end', seems extremely relevant to the second interpretation of liberal education, as general education. It is relevant because there are

three types of problem which any advocate of general education has to face and some kind of answer to them is provided
within this sphere of knowledge. There is first of all the problem of avoiding an assemblage of disjointed information;
there is second Herbert Spencer's question 'What knowledge
is of most worth?'; third there is the demand for 'integration'
that lurks behind talk of developing 'the whole man'. I will,
therefore, on occasions, make reference back to this sphere
of knowledge which is relevant to any person, in dealing with
these three types of problem in relation to which ambiguities
arise in the second interpretation of 'liberal education'.

(i) The demand that people should be allowed to develop
in many directions rather than be confined to some particular
specialized way of thinking is straightforward in a negative
sense, though the constraining enemy appears in many guises
ranging from the academic pedant to the demands of government or industry for specialized manpower. But the positive
implications are obscure. It is clear that a man should not be,
for instance, just a narrowly trained scientist, but should he
be philosophically sophisticated as well as aesthetically sensitive and well versed in history? How coarsely or finely are
such divisions to be made if illiberal specialization is to be
avoided? Does it matter, for instance, if a scientist supple-
ments his outlook by a developed appreciation of music, but
misses out on literature? Or what if the literary man understands the second law of thermo-dynamics but misses out on
Mendel, Freud, and Durkheim?

To answer this kind of question it must surely be insisted
that this conception of liberal education suggests only a continuum at one end of which is narrow specialization. It would
be impossible to locate any particular point on the move
away from this towards the other end of breadth of understanding and sensitivity, at which a person could be called
'educated'. Also some view would have to be taken, such as
that of Hirst, about the arbitrariness or non-arbitrariness of
divisions within knowledge. In the history of philosophy
there has been a gradual differentiation. Empirical science
was shown not to be just a branch of mathematics because
of the difference in its criterion of truth and testing procedures. For similar reasons moral experience was shown to be

unassimilable to either mathematics or science, to have a degree of autonomy. Questions then arose about the status of religion and about the possibility of regarding human studies such as psychology and history as similar to or distinct from the natural sciences. And both aesthetic appreciation and philosophical understanding seemed also to have *sui generis* characteristics.

If such non-arbitrary distinctions could be made in terms of truth-criteria, testing procedures and distinctive conceptual schemes, some beginning could be made to answering questions about the ideal implicit in the continuum. It would be absurd to expect, for instance, that in all these various disciplines a person should be able to operate the testing procedures in the way in which a trained specialist, who helps to develop understanding, must operate them. On the other hand it would not seem desirable for a person to amass a store of disjointed information from a variety of disciplines. What would seem desirable and practicable over a long period of time would be that a person should acquire essential elements of the different conceptual schemes by means of which various items of information are given a place and organized. He should also learn to apply this scheme critically, which implies understanding of the different criteria of truth. Understanding of principles would be attempted which would increasingly structure a person's outlook and help him to organize experience in a variety of ways, and to think critically and imaginatively.

(ii) With the vast development of knowledge in all these different disciplines questions would obviously arise, about which branches to single out for study within them. Within natural science, for instance, should chemistry be studied rather than astronomy? In other words the question of what knowledge is of most worth would have to be faced. If there is any substance in the points made before about the sort of knowledge which is relevant to anyone who has to face the general conditions of human life, some kind of answer could be sketched. In this sense within philosophy, for instance, ethics would obviously be more relevant than symbolic logic; within history social history would be more relevant than diplomatic history. And so on.

This, of course, is not the only criterion for including studies in a curriculum. There are many others. I am merely drawing attention to an important criterion of the 'worth' of knowledge that is too often overlooked by teachers who see subjects merely as first stages in specialized study. At universities, too, an important consideration for any teacher is what there is in his subject for the majority who have neither the aptitude nor the inclination to develop it as a research worker like himself. The neglect, however, of this criterion both in schools and universities underlies much of the complaint by students of the lack of 'relevance' in their studies.

(iii) The third type of problem implicit in general education is that of how all-round understanding is to be conceived. One facet of this ideal is the capacity of a person to view what he is doing or what is going on under different aspects. A scientist for instance, should not be oblivious to the moral dimension of his work; an engineer should be sensitive to the aesthetic aspect of his constructions. But more than this is often implied; for the different ways of organizing experience should not be compartmentalized and insulated from each other. There should be some kind of 'integration' between them. This is not the place to explore the different things which might be meant by 'integration' in this context, but one very pertinent meaning is the way in which different types of understanding interpenetrate in the spheres of knowledge which are relevant to anyone facing the general conditions of human life. In dealing with death, for instance, there is empirical knowledge about man's mortality, but this is inescapably tinged with philosophical assumptions about the relationship between consciousness and its bodily conditions. There are also inescapable ethico-religious questions about what is to be made of this universal predicament. The same sorts of considerations apply to confrontations with human violence or deceit. There are first of all straightforward factual questions about the actions. But these quickly shade into further questions about the motives of the person or persons concerned. And it is significant that motives such as envy, jealousy, and greed do not just explain; they are also the names of widespread vices. Moral judgment and interpersonal understanding are inextricably interwoven. And both

61

types of knowledge are exercised within a context of beliefs of varying levels of sophistication about how society works.

My point is not just that in this sphere problems seldom turn up that can be neatly labelled 'empirical' or 'ethical' or 'requiring understanding of persons'. It is also that there is a widespread interpenetration between the forms of understanding that we employ to sort out the specific aspects of problems. There are links, though tenuous ones, between pure mathematics and moral understanding. But pure mathematics has little purchase in this realm. There are, however, countless links between moral knowledge and interpersonal understanding, both of which have ubiquitous application to it. So the sphere in which it is easy to make some sense of the notion of the integration of forms of knowledge is the sphere in which it is possible to give at least one type of answer to the question 'Which knowledge is of most worth?'.

4 Liberal education as the development of the free man

In the classical view of liberal education the assumption was that movement towards the natural end of rationality was self-originated, the development of a potentiality immanent in any individual. Processes of education provided support and encouragement. The 'free man', on the Platonic view at any rate, was the man whose reason was properly in control, who was not constrained by unruly passions. Modern variants of this ideal stress different aspects of it without its underlying doctrine of function which assigned a universal end to human development. They are more individualistic in that they envisage different ends for different men. But they share the belief that it is of crucial importance that the individual should choose what he is to become.

Extreme versions of modern individualism stress the importance of everyone doing his own thing, of being 'true to himself'. Self-origination is interpreted in terms of authenticity, of not copying others or conforming to social roles, whether of being a woman or being a waiter. Thus any processes of education which involve being told things by others, being initiated into public traditions, or being influenced by example, are thought of as constricting on the individual's development. He must find his own way by his own experience and discoveries and eventually learn to be himself, do his own thing, even, in some versions of this doctrine, construct his own reality.

Less extreme and more intelligible versions of individualism, which are usually put forward by people who would not mind calling themselves liberals, combine this stress on individual choice with an equal stress on the role of reason in informing such choices. The emphasis is on autonomy as well as on authenticity. In other words the importance of first-hand experience, of beliefs which are not second hand, and codes of conduct that are not accepted just on authority, is granted. But stress is placed on the role of reason in achieving such independence of mind. On this view the development of the free-man[7] is not necessarily impeded by instruction from others, by public traditions and the example of others. Indeed it would be argued that the development of mind is inexplicable without reference to such social transactions which the extreme liberal regards as restrictions. What is crucial is the encouragement of criticism in the individual so that he can eventually accept or reject what he hears, sees, or is told on the basis of reasons. What is inimical to such development is any process, such as indoctrination or conditioning, which inhibits or undermines the capacity to reason.

This third interpretation of liberal education brings to the fore again the question about the type of knowledge which is of most worth, which was raised in relation to the two other interpretations. For, if autonomy is to be anything more than a pious hope, the individual must be possessed of relevant information to make realistic choices and have his imagination stimulated so that he can envisage all sorts of possibilities. In addition to specialized knowledge necessary for the pursuit of a particular occupation the individual will need various types of general knowledge which are relevant to his choices as a citizen and as a human being. In such general education too little attention is given to political education and what any individual should know who is to make informed choices as a citizen in a democracy. Too little attention, also, is given to that body of knowledge that bears directly on the general conditions of human life which has been referred to previously in this article. The Schools Council Humanities Project is one of the few attempts to connect the development of understanding in crucial areas such as those of violence, law and order, sex and personal relationships, with the development of autonomy. Many may have doubts about its emphasis on the 'neutrality' of the teacher, though this has to be understood against the tendency for teachers to indoctrinate their pupils on such controversial issues. But this emphasis of the project on a particular sort of teaching procedure must be separated from its emphasis on the importance of understanding in certain areas to the development of autonomy.

There may seem to be some inconsistency between this ideal of autonomy and what was said about the unrealistic tendency to think of pupils as potential research workers in the context of the first and second interpretations of liberal education. This is a vast topic about which it is possible, in the space available, to make only a few brief points. The first is that autonomy is very much a matter of degree; it indicates an attitude of mind rather than an achieved state. Knowledge has developed to such an extent in so many specialized branches, many of which impinge on our daily lives, that we have little alternative but to take a great deal of it on trust. Also, even in a sphere such as the moral one, the lives of reasonably autonomous people are governed by all sorts of rules on which they have reflected little. How many English people, for instance, have pondered deeply on the ethics of 'first come, first served' in queues? Most people are brought up in some established way of behaving and reflect on various elements of it in the light of their developing experience. The liberal ideal of autonomy is to be understood in contrast to unthinking conformity and rigid adherence to dogma. It does not demand making explicit everything which has been picked up from various sources and subjecting it all to constant criticism. What it does require is a willingness to learn and to revise opinions and assumptions when confronted with situations that challenge them. Logically speaking, too, criticism must take certain presuppositions for granted. Not everything can be questioned at once.

Second, it is important to distinguish approaching what one is told critically and attempting to organize and synthesize what one hears or reads in one's own way, from either slavishly reproducing the views of some authority on the one hand or developing a highly original thesis on the other. Autonomy is most frequently associated with the moral sphere; but few people who attain a fair degree of autonomy in their moral life are moral innovators. This introduces the third point which is that there are great differences in respect of being able to manage without authorities in the various ways of thinking that are relevant to the sphere of knowledge which is of central importance to any human being. In the natural sciences, in so far as they impinge on everyday life, most people perforce rely on authorities. They may get as far as understanding some of the underlying theory; they realize that it is subject to error; but very few have the necessary training to locate possible sources of error. Morals are very different; for its underlying principles are not particularly recondite and a highly specialized training is not necessary to be sensitive to them. What is needed is the judgment and imagination to apply them in varying circumstances. There is also the problem of the degree of weight attached to different principles which is one of the most potent sources of moral controversy. In between fall the various branches of human studies in which the 'common sense' understanding of others and of ourselves is illuminated by theories supplied by specialized disciplines such as psychology, economics, and sociology. In assessing such theories, or the interpretations of actions and policies which they provide, the knowledge of particular men acting and suffering in particular circumstances is of crucial importance. We all possess such knowledge in various degrees; so we have a shared basis for criticism, judgment and making our own syntheses of what we glean from various 'authorities'. We have, of course, to be sufficiently 'on the inside' of such disciplines to understand the structure of their principles and how to apply them. But we do not have to be specialists in them in order to form some view of our own.

What emerges from this sketchy piece of probing is the need for more careful attention to a group of qualities associated with autonomy such as being critical, being independent, having judgment, being authentic, being imaginative and so on. The application of these in spheres such as those of morals and politics, understanding other people, professional skill, etc., needs to be studied as well as in more academic spheres where they are often used for assessing students' work. These are to be distinguished from more mundane qualities such as being well informed and showing understanding on the one hand and more exalted qualities such as being original, creative, and inventive on the other. In so far as liberal education is concerned with autonomy it obviously aims at getting people beyond the level of just understanding and being well informed. But it does not demand the other extreme of originality and creativeness. Such qualities are extremely important for university teachers who are training specialists likely to advance knowledge, but they are an extra bonus for liberal educators concerned with the development of autonomy.

Conclusion

This paper really has no conclusions. This is partly because its intention was not to reach any but to explore some of the ambiguities inherent in liberal education. But it is also because, as the exploration proceeded, I began to feel an increasing dissatisfaction with the dichotomies in terms of which liberal education is usually interpreted. In particular I found difficulty with the dichotomy between 'for its own sake' and for the sake of some practical end which seems to me to have application to the advancement of knowledge but to fit very loosely over its acquisition. It seems to apply hardly at all to a sphere of knowledge, sometimes referred to loosely as 'the humanities', which is of central importance in any attempt to determine the type of knowledge which should form the content of liberal education. Having come to the end of this paper, therefore, I really feel that I should now get down to the very difficult task of trying to delimit this type of knowledge more precisely, examine its relationship to traditional disciplines, to vocational studies, and so on. But this might mean that the paper would become only marginally concerned with 'liberal education' as it is normally understood, even though it might be 'liberal' in exemplifying the untrammelled pursuit of knowledge. And it would certainly become too 'liberal' in its length.

Notes

1 My thanks are due to Paul Hirst, whose constructive criticisms helped me to revise a first version of this paper.
2 See R. S. Peters, *Ethics and Education*, London, Allen & Unwin, 1966, pp. 43–5.
3 See P. H. Hirst, 'Liberal Education and the Nature of Knowledge', most easily available as reprinted in R. S. Peters (ed.), *The Philosophy of Education*, Oxford University Press, 1973, pp. 87–111.
4 See Mary Warnock, 'Towards a Definition of Quality in Education' in R. S. Peters (ed.), *The Philosophy of Education*, Oxford University Press, 1973, pp. 112–22.
5 See *ibid*.
6 See A. N. Whitehead, *The Aims of Education*, New York, Mentor Books, 1949, p. 16.
7 For detailed development of such a view see R. S. Peters, 'Freedom and the Development of the Free-Man' in J. Doyle (ed.), *Educational Judgements*, London, Routledge & Kegan Paul, 1973. Reprinted in R. S. Peters, *Psychology and Ethical Development*, London, Allen & Unwin, 1974.

4　Dilemmas in liberal education

Introduction

The liberal always has an uncomfortable time as soon as he addresses himself to the problem of implementing his favoured ideal of freedom. To start with there is the well-known 'paradox of freedom' which points to the necessity of acceptance of the rule of law to protect individuals in spheres where their pursuit of individual interest is vulnerable to interference from other arbitrary individuals or to group pressures. The levelling constraints of law have to be accepted by all to safeguard the individual against grosser interferences with his individual interests. Second, liberals usually accept other values such as those of justice and the welfare of others. On occasions, therefore, a case can be made for scaling down claims deriving from freedom because of considerations falling under these other principles. Third, individuals seldom pursue their interests in isolation. They take part in activities which demand certain ground rules. When these activities become institutionalized the rules necessary for the effective pursuit and perpetuation of the activity come to be felt as oppressive in relation to the point of the activity. Protesters jib at the constraints of protestantism. Thus the liberal is constantly confronted with difficulties and dilemmas arising from various features of situations in which he has to implement his ideal.

In this paper I propose to explore this theme in the particular case of various ideals of 'liberal education'. I say 'various ideals' because liberal education is no one thing. The unifying conception is that of the untrammelled development of the mind. But there are different views, dominant at different times, about what constrains such development. At the moment liberal education is thought of as being more or less equivalent to general education.[1] This is a protest, starting in

68

the nineteenth century, against the growing specialization and compartmentalization of knowledge. The demand is for the mind to be allowed to develop in different directions instead of being confined to one discipline or specialized form of understanding, which is thought of as restriction. In the Greek ideal of liberal education, however, the restriction was seen much more as deriving from the harnessing of knowledge to practical ends. The doctrine of 'essence' proclaimed that the end of man is the development of reason. Theoretical pursuits were regarded as the most pure and perfect form of this development. So the pursuit of knowledge 'for its own sake' emerged as an ideal to be contrasted with the instrumental pursuit of knowledge for more mundane ends. Finally liberal education is sometimes understood as a protest against constrictions on the mind's development occasioned by dogmatic methods of teaching or authoritarian ways of organizing the context of learning. This kind of protest is now very fashionable. Indeed de-schoolers see schooling itself as the main enemy of individual development, though actually they would probably jib at being described as liberals.

I have examined elsewhere[2] the ambiguities inherent in these three interpretations of liberal education. In this paper I will assume a rough and ready understanding of what is meant; for this will be sufficient to deal with its main theme which is that of the difficulties and dilemmas with which the liberal is confronted when trying to implement all three interpretations of the liberal ideal.

1   Liberal education as general education

The dilemma of the liberal in relation to the interpretation of liberal education as general education is caricatured by those who maintain that the ideal of the educated man is as anachronistic as that of the courtly knight. Facts of institutionalization and individual psychology, it is argued, make it attainable only by the few; yet the modern liberal is likely to be sensitive to considerations of fairness and so may feel embarrassed about pressing for it if he accepts the institutional analysis and psychological arguments of such critics.

The fundamental difficulty in dealing with this question is

the lack of clarity in what the liberal is advocating. It is clear that he is opposed to narrow specialization but his positive ideal is very indeterminate. A man should not be just a highly trained scientist, but should he be philosophically sophisticated as well as steeped in literature and history? If he has to be aesthetically sensitive, as well as scientifically trained, is a literary background enough? Can he miss out on music and on the visual arts? Similarly, does it matter if the literary man misses out on Freud and Max Weber if he masters the second law of thermo-dynamics? Suppose that some version of the 'forms of knowledge'[3] thesis is accepted, according to which there are non-arbitrary distinctions within knowledge because of distinctive types of concepts and truth-criteria (e.g. science, maths, morals), how deeply immersed has a liberally educated person to become in each of them? Is it sufficient for the literary person to be knowledgeable about science or history? Or does he have to be able to assess some of the evidence on which conclusions are based? If so how many forms of understanding is it realistic to suppose that an average student could begin to explore at secondary school level?

The vast development of knowledge in all its forms makes this question of content even more acute. For even if it was conceded that all-round understanding could be divided into between six and ten main 'forms of knowledge' (depending on how finely or coarsely various distinctions are made) there would then be the question of e.g. which science was of central importance to an educated person or whether social history was more relevant than constitutional or economic history, whether one had to know any ancient or European history. And so on. I have argued elsewhere that insufficient attention has been given to Herbert Spencer's question 'What knowledge is of most worth?'[4] He asked this in the nineteenth century, when specialization was gathering momentum. It is a crucial question for anyone defending this interpretation of liberal education in the twentieth century. For unless some central core of all-round understanding can be defined, which it is not unrealistic for the average individual to attain by the end of the secondary stage of schooling, the liberal is wide open to the charge that his ideal is an elitist one.

Even if this preliminary condition is met there are still difficulties in implementing it deriving from facts of institutionalization and individual psychology. The institutional difficulties spring really from the basic reason for having special institutions such as schools in the first place, which is because of the specialized character of the knowledge necessary for an industrialized society to perpetuate itself and for the individual to make something of himself within it. At the lowest level there is the basic numeracy and literacy necessary for information and instructions to be disseminated and assimilated and for economic life to proceed. At the highest level there is training for the professions such as law, medicine, and engineering and training of research workers for the advancement of knowledge. In the middle is training in various branches of technical knowledge necessary for manufacture, maintenance and public services. As these institutions will have to be financed mainly out of public funds there will be an insistence that all achieve a basic level of numeracy and literacy and that the occupational structure is adequately served in respect of its need for specialized man-power. This may be done by central control or in various other ways. But whichever way it is done the logic of the situation is such that there is likely to be an emphasis on specialization. This may be supplemented, as in communist or Catholic countries, by some ideological instruction thought necessary for citizenship, but, from the State's point of view the development of all-round understanding, as advocated by the liberal, is bound to seem a bit of a luxury. Witness the anomalous position of 'liberal studies' in technical colleges.

There is also the further point that the institutions at the apex of the pyramid, i.e. universities and polytechnics, are very costly to maintain, and, with the growth of knowledge, more and more demands are made on their research and teaching resources. They, therefore, quite naturally expect more and more of the preparatory work to be done by students at school and arrange their entrance requirements accordingly. The schools can only meet these requirements by early specialization and this is bound to be at the expense of general education. The alternative of spreading out the whole process over a greater length of time is only available

71

to countries with vast resources to spend on schooling.

These institutional obstacles to liberal education are strengthened, so it is argued, by psychological deficiencies in motivation. Pupils tend to work at things either if they can see some practical outcome or if they get interested in them for their own sake. The practical outcome of most specialized studies is obvious enough — a place in a university or polytechnic, a job, or a profession. But is there any similar practical outcome to a general education? Maybe, too, they may become interested in one or two subjects for their own sake. But it is most improbable that they will develop much enthusiasm for work if they are trying to understand too many things at once. So it is pointless to bore them interminably in the interests of a liberal education.

These psychological arguments, like the initial objection that liberal education can only be possible for the few, are telling in the absence of any clear view about its content. If, for instance, it were accepted that it should be centred round a range of questions arising from the general conditions of human life — e.g. palpable phenomena of the natural world such as the dark, storms, the tides, time, changes of the seasons, problematic phenomena of the social world such as authority, violence, suffering, ownership, people's reactions to other people, the cycle of birth, marriage, and death, and so on — then the attitude of students to it might be different. This kind of content might provide the 'relevance' which they so often claim to be lacking. Certainly, too, the dichotomy in motivation between studying something for its practical use or for its own sake seems altogether too crude to cover possible motivations to learn, as I shall argue later.

There is finally the dilemma which faces the liberal about how he is to ensure an adequate general education even supposing that he lived in a more ideal world; for to date I have been drawing attention to actual impediments in the world as it is. Formally speaking, in the English educational system, the curriculum of the secondary school is the responsibility of the governors of schools subject to general advice from Local Education Authorities. In practice this means that the headmaster has a considerable degree of autonomy which is in fact circumscribed by public examinations for the content of which the universities have a major responsibility. Suppose that, in order to avoid the specialization that this link with universities seems to bring in its train, this system were abandoned. What alternative would there be to guidelines for the curriculum from the central government in order to avoid the probable anarchy, unfairness, parochialism and possible political bias of leaving it just to Local Authorities and teachers to determine their own? And would not such centralized control of the curriculum be repugnant to anyone of liberal persuasions? He objects to the mind being constricted by being confined to specialized study. But would he not also object to state direction which laid down too definitely the other directions in which it was desirable for the mind to develop? And would not, in any case, such centralized direction tend to favour those specialized forms of knowledge that it is in the interest of the state to encourage?

2 Liberal education as knowledge for its own sake

There are similar obscurities, difficulties, and dilemmas in any attempt to implement the ideal of liberal education when it is interpreted as knowledge for its own sake. It has to be asked, first, what this ideal amounts to in ordinary situations of learning in schools. It manifestly has application in universities which are concerned, to a large extent, with the advancement of knowledge. It can be claimed that there are values in the developments of knowledge itself which constitute reasons for its advancement. Research need not always be justified in terms of its benefit to the community or its usefulness to the professions. These different reasons for research are obvious enough in universities. The liberal stresses the importance of these values which are intrinsic to knowledge; and in this context his ideal has obvious application.

The ideal, however, becomes a bit obscure when it is transferred to educational situations which are more concerned with the acquisition of knowledge than with its advancement. To start with, to what is learning 'for its own sake' opposed? If a pupil practises feverishly on a violin because he wants to win a prize, he is manifestly learning for some extrinsic reason. A great deal of learning at school is of this character. Work has to be done to pass examinations which count as entry tickets to a range of well-paid or prestigious occupations. There is no close connexion between the performances required in the occupations and what is learnt, though many might argue that certain studies such as English and mathematics contain necessary skills for working in any occupation at a certain level. But suppose that the pupil wanted to be a violinist or wanted to play a sonata which he could not play without mastering the type of fingering which he was practising? Would he then be learning something 'for its own sake'?

There is no clear answer to this question because the dichotomy between 'for its own sake' and 'for the sake of some further end' is too coarse to deal with situations of learning. 'Learning' is inseparable from a variety of achievements, depending on what is being learnt. There are logical links of various kinds between these achievements and the learning experiences that lead up to them. Learning to play various passages is constitutive of having mastered a sonata. Learning to play in the third position is a necessary condition of being able to play these passages. And particular passages instantiate the values of precision, expressiveness, and so on, of the work as a whole. Similarly the over-all end of being a violinist includes within it the values immanent in playing various works, including Handel sonatas. The same sort of points could be made about practical activities like tool-making or medicine or theoretical activities like science. So if one is talking about motivations to learn, and talking of particular segments of learning, it is clear that 'for its own sake' rules out toiling away with thoughts only about obtaining cash or approval. But it is not clear what it rules in. Obviously if a person is absorbed in every minute of practice, or finds every stage of a mathematical demonstration absorbing or fascinating, he is doing something 'for its own sake'. But what if he is attracted by the over-all activity of science, tool-making, or playing the violin, but finds parts of the necessary learning tedious or trying? Or suppose that he loves certain parts of a sonata but finds other parts tedious.

It might well be said that the notion of 'doing something for its own sake' applies to doing the activity as a whole rather than to learning it bit by bit and that these objections are quibbles. But if that is so what has this notion got to do with education, which is essentially connected with learning spread out in sequences over time? It takes a long time for most activities to be mastered sufficiently for the learner to see where the parts fit in and why certain things are necessary, as well as to appreciate fully the various values which the activity instantiates. Furthermore, when applied to activities, ever since the Greeks, the distinction has been used to contrast pursuing *knowledge* for its own sake with pursuing it for practical ends. But this is ambiguous; for 'practical ends' include both ends such as the relief of suffering which are intrinsic to a practical activity such as medicine, as well as the obtaining of cash or prestige which can influence doctors as well as scientists engaged in the pursuit of knowledge 'for its own sake'. Practical ends, in other words, can be both intrinsic or extrinsic to activities.

I have argued that the liberal ideal of 'knowledge for its own sake' has more obvious application to institutions for the advancement of knowledge, such as universities, than to institutions such as schools, which are concerned mainly with its acquisition. Nevertheless, it has some application to schools. Given that pupils get a certain way in a subject they can come to enjoy it for what it opens up to them and study it 'for its own sake'. Indeed there are some, such as Mary Warnock,[5] who hold that this is one of the main arguments for specialization. At a very early age, too, children can be stimulated to learn by phenomena which awaken their curiosity. They may be presented with challenges which appeal to their desire to master things. This is the type of motivation which the liberal advocates at school level, and undoubtedly it is extremely important in education.

The liberal, however, must be, to a certain extent, assailed by doubts and confronted by dilemmas if he wishes to concentrate on implementing this ideal. To start with the doubts. Is he extolling this as the *only* desirable form of motivation? Or is he drawing attention to it as a form of motivation that is only too likely to be forgotten in a society like our own, which makes it difficult to develop, as I shall soon show. If he is doing the former, what arguments are there for maintaining its overriding value, in the absence of some equivalent of the old Greek doctrine of function which accorded supreme value to the theoretical life? If a medical student devotes himself to the study of anatomy and physiology, which he may find boring, because he genuinely wishes to relieve suffering and views this knowledge as necessary to this end, why should his study lack value? He will have to have some concern for truth, which is a valuative aspect of any pursuit of knowledge. Indeed, the thought that if his beliefs are erroneous, his patients may suffer, gives additional point to it, though, of course, the value of truth cannot be defended entirely by reference to its contribution to human benefit. He may wish to draw attention to values intrinsic to attempts to understand the world, but why should he be impervious to other values intrinsic to trying to change it for the better? Why should hedonistic values in particular, such as enjoyment and satisfaction, have the inner track?

The liberal may be objecting to the all-pervasive influence of extrinsic ends which corrupt the acquisition of theoretical and practical knowledge. And in this he is confronted by dilemmas partly deriving from institutionalizing the acquisition of knowledge in a consumption-orientated type of society and partly from facts of human psychology.

In an advanced industrial society there is a limit to the amount of direct vocational preparation that can go on at school. The boy who wishes to be a toolmaker will not usually be rigorously examined in his manual skills by the firm that interviews him. More likely evidence will be sought of his level of mastery in English, mathematics and elementary physics. The firm will prefer to do its own technical training at work in conjunction with a neighbouring technical college which may provide it. Whether this divorce of the secondary school from a *direct* link with the occupational structure is desirable is another question. On the one hand it is argued that, in our system, there should be a merger between the later stages of secondary education and further education, which provides most of the technical training at this level. On the other hand it is objected that too tight a link between the school and the occupational structure will determine people's life chances too early. Too many will be singled out too soon as modern equivalents of hewers of wood and drawers of water and conditioned against conceiving of any other possibility.

Whatever the desirability of linking the school more directly with occupations the fact is that the link tends to be, in the main, indirect. What is provided is a public examination system which is thought to give some indication of a person's general level of attainment in literacy and numeracy. The school thus acts as a selecting and grading agency for determining people's general ability and aptitude so that they can be slotted in at an appropriate level in the occupational structure. From society's point of view this ensures an appropriate flow of manpower to the various levels of the occupational structure. And examinations will be seen by the individual as the main determinants of his life chances. Little relationship will be seen between what is being studied at school and later life. So the situation of the boy working at metalwork because he wants to be a toolmaker will not be a common one. The liberal, too, is likely to flourish in a society whose belief in the value of individual liberty is likely to manifest itself in competition and other distressing features of the rat-race. These will influence schooling which will be seen starkly as a ladder to success, status and wealth. Indeed, the school itself will reflect the values of society as a whole in which questions like 'where does it get you?' and 'what is the pay-off?' are asked about almost anything.

Philosophers and psychologists have argued from the beginning of time about the universality and strength of such self-regarding motives as envy, greed, and ambition. Whatever their status as part of the fabric of 'human nature' they are obviously likely to be encouraged in a society which values individual liberty and self-realization. Motivation is not just something which the individual brings with him to social situations. It is, in part, a product of those very situations, of what is expected of him in a given context. If the school, like industry, is structured in terms of individual attainment, measured by public examinations, this is the message that the individual is likely to read off from his learning situation. Teachers may try to get pupils to work for the love of their subjects. They may extol the values of 'knowledge for its own sake'. But the pupils, even if they admire them, treat them only semi-seriously. For the institution is issuing quite different directives to them. They are therefore likely to be as 'alienated' from their learning as are workers in a capitalist society who get no joy and take no pride in their work, but who clock in just for the cash, and get by with standards of work that do not lead to disapproval or dismissal.

The institutional situation of the student may well be reinforced by the existence of developmental levels of motivation. Piaget, when dealing with moral development, distinguished the early ego-centric stage of a child's attitude to rules, when he sees them as ways of avoiding punishment and obtaining rewards, from the second stage when he sees them as things to be done in order to gain approval or avoid disapproval, and the final stage when he can see rules more reflectively as alterable and negotiable, whose necessity depends on reasons which are not artificially tacked on like rewards or approval. Discipline gradually comes to be accepted because its relevance to the pursuit of felt concerns and interests is appreciated. It arises from common tasks, not from the attitudes of others to them. Now in learning various subjects and skills there may be features that are immediately interesting, puzzling, and attractive, which appeal to children at a quite early stage. But after this initial period of what Whitehead calls 'romance', there is a period of 'precision' when the student has to get to grips with the standards of the subject. At a certain stage he may be unable to see the point of mastering what is demanded of him in relation to the subject itself. If he is to overcome his counter-inclinations it may well be that some extrinsic motivation such as that provided by approval or reward is necessary. The hope is that he will gradually come to be drawn in a different way to the subject once he gets more on the inside of it and becomes sensitive to the relationship between its standards and immanent values. Thus extrinsic motivation may prove an important source of transitional inducements.

The difficulties and dilemmas of the liberal in relation to the interpretation of liberal education as 'knowledge for its own sake' have now been explained. He is likely to flourish in a society in which the values of individualism are likely to provide extrinsic motives which are inimical to knowledge for its own sake; this institutional situation may well be reinforced by facts about the development of motivation. To what extent, then, is it advisable for him to employ extrinsic motivation in the hope that various forms of intrinsic motivation may take over? Given that motivation is, to a large extent, socially conditioned, he is likely to meet in school a large number of children who have no interest in learning and who are strangers to the joys of enquiry. Maybe curiosity is innate in man, but sociological findings suggest that it can be massively discouraged by certain types of home background. How then is the liberal to deal with this type of practical situation which is so widespread in modern industrial societies? Is he to employ the stock forms of extrinsic motivation in the hope that eventually those who work in the first place to obtain approval, to pass examinations, and to get on in the world may develop some delight in doing at least some things for their own sake? Or is his main hope to relate learning to 'practical ends' that are far removed in time but intrinsically related to the learning, as in the case of the boy doing metalwork to become a toolmaker? Or are there a host of things as I have elsewhere suggested,[6] that are eagerly learnt but which are not obviously learnt either for their own sake or for the sake of some practical end? Is it this type of motivation in learning that lies behind a lot of the current student demand for relevance? Is the trouble with this interpretation of 'liberal education', as I have suggested, that 'knowledge for its own sake' can easily be applied to the advancement of knowledge but only tangentially to its acquisition?

3 Liberal education as non-authoritarian education

The third interpretation of 'liberal education' emphasizes the development of individual choice culminating in the achievement of autonomy — the independence of mind of the 'freeman'. It is to be contrasted both with conformity or accepting opinions and attitudes unthinkingly from others, and with more drastic ways in which an individual can be programmed by others — e.g. indoctrination. More positively it suggests authenticity and self-origination. Beliefs and actions must be one's own, not copied from others or the product of role-playing. It also, in most versions of it, suggests a critical appraisal of beliefs and practices and the development of independence of mind as a result.

On the face of it compulsory schooling itself is an inauspicious beginning for a liberal who is trying to implement such an ideal. A liberal would not be sympathetic to the argument that this interference with liberty is necessary so that the state can be assured of an adequate supply of trained manpower. But he would appreciate the necessity for the individual to have knowledge and skill both for occupational purposes and for the individual to acquire those products of his cultural heritage which will help him to see significance in the context in which he has to live his life. In particular he will appreciate that the liberal ideal of autonomy for the individual will be empty unless his capacity for choice is enlarged by information, imagination, and critical thought. Unless, therefore, an individual is definitely put in the way of relevant studies in literature, history, geography and parts of the natural and social sciences, he may be severely handicapped in respect of many of the choices which he may have to make.[7]

But why, it might well be asked, should individuals be *compelled* to attend special institutions where, if they are lucky, they will be put in the way of such relevant knowledge? Why should they not attend them voluntarily or join the 'learning webs' advocated by Illich? Why would not the liberal obviously favour such proposals for liberation? Because he probably believes also in fairness and appreciates what would almost certainly happen if attendance at such institutions were left to the decision of the individual, which would mean, in effect, to that of his parents. For those who would avail themselves of opportunities to learn would be those who come from homes in which they already get strong encouragement. Such a voluntary system would tend to heap a cumulative disadvantage on those who, because of their home background, are already disadvantaged. Perhaps, however, a liberal might advocate a radical revision of secondary education in which this was no longer seen just as a stepping stone to an occupation or to higher education. Rather it should be conceived of as a level of experience open to everyone but not rigidly confined to the age of adolescence. Some of the voluntary spirit of the adult education movement might thus be infused into it, in which a great variety of students attend classes out of interest or because they see the relevance to their lives of what they are studying. In our system this would mean an extension of the community educational centre idea in which what we now call further and adult education would take place on both a part-time and full-time basis as well as the type of learning more usually associated with the secondary school.

However, for people to take advantage even of such reformed institutions at secondary level, compulsory attendance would be necessary at primary and early secondary level. And, even if attendance were voluntary, once a special institution devoted to learning is instituted, the situation is fraught with paradoxes from the point of view of the development of autonomy. For the learning situation of the young person is one in which he is being initiated into a public inheritance. He cannot have a mind of his own unless he makes sense of his experience through public concepts that permit communication. The world which he learns to inhabit is a construction determined, in part, by the shared beliefs of his parents and teachers. So there must be a long period in the life of a human being when his beliefs and conduct are emphatically not autonomous; for he has laboriously to become the sort of being who can entertain beliefs that fit the world and forms of conduct that enable him to negotiate his way in social life. This heteronomous situation lasts for a long time. Indeed, in the view of followers of Piaget, most of the human race never emerge from it. Autonomy is very much the product of individualistic societies in which there is an emphasis on reciprocity, seeing the other person's point of view, finding out things for oneself and being the determiner of one's own destiny. In most societies the appeal to authorities, or conformity to public opinion, is the predominant source of beliefs and conduct.

The situation of the learner in special institutions is equally unpromising from the point of view of autonomy. For, whether they are voluntary or compulsory, they exist because the knowledge that has to be transmitted is not available in the home. So people attend them because they are ignorant and those who teach in them are meant to be authorities of some sort on what it is thought necessary for people to know. Also, if a lot of people have to learn in a small place, various authoritative devices have to be used to permit conditions of learning because of the relevance of the 'paradox of freedom' to this context. Also, in compulsory institutions, given the lack of motivation of many, forms of extrinsic motivation such as praise and blame, rewards and punishment have to be employed to encourage the reluctant to learn. For these are the only forms of motivation that are effective for people at the heteronomous stage. Thus the control and motivational structure of the institution, because it has to cater predominantly for people who are not autonomous in their conduct and motivation, is unlikely to provide a climate in which autonomy is encouraged.

The dilemma of the liberal is therefore plain enough. How can an individual be encouraged to think for himself when he is placed in a situation in which he has to learn from others and whose control and motivational structures have to cater for those who are reluctant to learn? This type of dilemma, perhaps, is not so difficult to dissolve as the two previous ones. The first general point to make is that certain procedures, while not being particularly liberal, are not manifestly illiberal either. Most of the things we learn we pick up from other people in various ways. We do not discover them for ourselves and we may not be particularly eager to learn them. Nevertheless we learn them. This only becomes an illiberal procedure if other people convey these things to us in such a way that we are discouraged from questioning them and if the method of instruction is such that it has a general tendency to discourage us to be curious or critical. There is no evidence to suggest that learning by the example or from the instruction of others, accompanied perhaps by praise when we get things right, necessarily has this indoctrinatory effect.

Romantics writing about education contrast the repressive methods of schooling with the 'natural' way in which people discover things for themselves when they are curious. But they overlook the main mechanism by means of which the human race has survived, which is that of imitation of and identification with, others who are more experienced. It is mainly through these mechanisms that cultural transmission takes place. Most of our early learning takes place in this way. It is unfortunate that these mechanisms are so neglected by those who are rightfully indignant about much of the goading and bribing that goes on in schools. Of course it is desirable to encourage spontaneous problem-solving and learning pursued out of individual interest, as Dewey did. But to suggest that *all* learning should take place in this way is not only impracticable, as supporters of the individual project method in schools discovered; it is also unnecessary, for it overlooks the way in which, from time immemorial, most beliefs and forms of conduct have been learnt by the human race, namely by picking them up from the example and in-struction of more experienced people who rank as authorities or experts in a community.

There are dangers, of course, of indoctrination in this type of learning. It is not just that teachers and other people who are authorities are often doctrinaire and dogmatic and pas-sionately want their pupils to think as they do. It is also that even those who regard their role as authorities as merely a transitional device for helping their pupils to learn, may have, quite unintentionally, a profound influence on them which fixates them with a set of beliefs. Their intention may be to initiate others into a form of thought in such a way that they may become critical and learn to think for themselves. But they may find, even after many years, that their pupils are still inordinately influenced by their views on particular issues. Thus the dilemma of the liberal is that one of the basic situations of learning, that of learning from others rather than from one's own experience, is non-liberal. But there is always a danger, in this authority type of situation, of its turning out illiberal, even if the experienced person is trying to encourage independent judgment in his pupils.

The same sort of point applies to the type of social con-trol necessary for a lot of people to learn together in a small space. Because of the paradox of freedom there must be rules enforced by someone in authority. But the system need not be authoritarian. The learners can co-operate in deciding what the rules shall be and in enforcing them. The trouble about authority in schools is that it has not yet been properly rationalized and adapted to the purposes of the school. It is basically paternalistic — a relic of a previous era.[8] Authority, whether in society generally or in a school, is not a liberal device. As it involves restriction on the individual it is something that always needs justification as a necessary nuisance to preserve either freedom or other values. But it only becomes positively illiberal when it is employed for no good reason or exercised in a way which is an affront to human dignity. Nevertheless, even if authority is rationalized and there is common acceptance of the rule-making and rule-enforcing procedures, they involve, by definition, restrictions on individual decision-making. Particular rules may be felt very strongly as constraints on their development by particular individuals. This is endemic to any rule-governed type of group activity. It should not be confused with extreme types of pressure on the individual characteristic of an authoritarian form of social control. Free-schoolers and de-schoolers seldom make this type of distinction.

Conclusion

In this paper no attempt has been made to justify liberal education. Indeed, as I have tried to show that 'liberal education' can mean very different things, different types of justification would presumably be required for the differing interpretations of it. Instead I have concentrated on the difficulties and dilemmas inherent in any attempt to implement three interpretations of liberal education. What emerges from this analysis is the necessity for much more thought on three main issues, which affect all three interpretations. What is required is:

(a) An answer to Herbert Spencer's question 'What knowledge is of most worth?'

(b) Attention to the institutionalization of education, especially at secondary level, so as to free it from pressures which strengthen premature specialization, the use of extrinsic motivation, and illiberal procedures of instruction and social control.

(c) An examination of teaching procedures so as to distinguish

84

those which are illiberal from those which are liberal and from those which, though not particularly liberal, are not manifestly illiberal.

Notes

1 See P. H. Hirst, 'Liberal Education and the Nature of Knowledge', most easily available as reprinted in R. S. Peters (ed.), *The Philosophy of Education*, Oxford University Press, 1973, pp. 87—111.
2 See chapter 3 above.
3 See P. H. Hirst, op. cit.
4 See chapter 3 above.
5 See Mary Warnock, 'Towards a Definition of Quality in Education' in R. S. Peters (ed.), op. cit.
6 See chapter 3 above.
7 For development of such arguments see R. S. Peters, *Ethics and Education*, London, Allen & Unwin, 1966, pp. 157—66 and 'The Justification of Education' in R. S. Peters (ed.), op. cit. See also J. P. White, *Towards a Compulsory Curriculum*, London, Routledge & Kegan Paul, 1973.
8 See R. S. Peters, *Authority, Responsibility and Education*, rev. ed., London, Allen & Unwin, 1973, ch. IV.

© R. S. Peters 1977

5   The justification of education

Introduction

To be educated is thought by many to be a desirable condition of mind, but it obviously does not encompass all that is desirable. Uneducated people can be compassionate and courageous and there is surely some value in such mental dispositions. On the other hand educated people often lack perseverance and sympathy, which are also generally thought to be valuable. So even though there may be value in being educated it must be associated with some specific types of value. What then are the values which are specific to being educated and what sort of justification can be given for them? It is to these limited questions that I propose to address myself in this article rather than to wider questions of value with which I was concerned in *Ethics and Education*, and with which, in places, I confused these limited questions — owing perhaps to certain inadequacies in the analysis of the concept of 'education' with which I was then working.

1   The values specific to education

What, then, are the values which are specific to being educated? This depends on whether 'education' is being used in a general or in a specific sense.[1] There is a general concept of 'education' which covers almost any process of learning, rearing, or bringing up. Nowadays, when we speak of education in this general way, we usually mean going to school, to an institution devoted to learning. In this sense of 'education' almost any quality of mind can be deemed a product of it — compassion and perseverance included. To say that such qualities of mind are the product of education is to say that they are learned. Education, in this sense, can be accorded any kind of instrumental value and so is not of any significance for its valuative suggestions.

Of more relevance is the specific concept of 'education' which emerged in the nineteenth century as a contrast to training. Various processes of learning came to be termed 'educative' because they contribute to the development of an educated man or woman. This was an ideal which emerged in opposition both to narrow specialization and to the increasingly instrumental view of knowledge associated with the development of technology. It was, of course, as old as the Greeks, though it was not previously picked out by the concept of an 'educated man'. Thus (*a*) the educated man is not one who merely possesses specialized skills. He may possess such specific know-how but he certainly also possesses a considerable body of knowledge together with understanding. He has a developed capacity to reason, to justify his beliefs and conduct. He knows the reason why of things as well as that certain things are the case. This is not a matter of just being knowledgeable; for the understanding of an educated person transforms how he sees things. It makes a difference to the level of life which he enjoys; for he has a backing for his beliefs and conduct and organizes his experience in terms of systematic conceptual schemes. (*b*) There is the suggestion, too, that his understanding is not narrowly specialized. He not only has breadth of understanding but is also capable of connecting up these different ways of interpreting his experience so that he achieves some kind of cognitive perspective. This can be exhibited in two sorts of ways. First he is not just embedded in one way of reacting to what he encounters. He can, for instance, combine a knowledge of how a car works with sensitivity to its aesthetic proportions, to its history, and to its potentiality for human good and ill. He can see it as a problem for town-planners as well as a fascinating machine. Second he is ready to pursue the links between the different sorts of understanding that he has developed. Any moral judgment, for instance, presupposes beliefs about people's behaviour and many moral judgments involve assessments of the consequences of behaviour. An educated person, therefore, will not rely on crude, unsophisticated interpretations of the behaviour of others when making moral judgments;

87

he will not neglect generalizations from the social sciences, in so far as they exist, about the probable consequences of types of behaviour. If these are at all sophisticated he will have to bring to bear some rudimentary understanding of statistics. Similarly, as a scientist he will not be oblivious of the moral presuppositions of scientific activity nor of the aesthetic features of theories; neither will he be insensitive to the relevance of his findings to wider issues of belief and action.

(c) In contrast, too, to the instrumentality so often associated with specialized knowledge, the educated person is one who is capable, to a certain extent, of doing and knowing things for their own sake. He can delight in what he is doing without always asking the question 'And where is this going to get me?' This applies as much to cooking as it does to chemistry. He can enjoy the company of a friend as well as a concert. And his work is not just a chore to be carried out for cash. He has a sense of standards as well as a sense of the setting of what he is doing between the past and the future. There are continuities in his life which reflect what he cares about. He takes care because he cares.

(d) Processes of education. These are forms of learning through which people become this way, by means of which they are gradually initiated into this form of life. They are not to be regarded strictly as means to being educated, if 'means' is taken as indicating a process which is both valuatively neutral and related to the end purely causally as taking a drug might be related to a tranquil state of mind. For these processes are processes of learning, and this always involves some kind of content to be mastered, understood, remembered. This content, whether it is a skill, an attitude, an item of knowledge, or a principle to be understood, must be intimated, perhaps in embryonic form, in the learning situation. There must, therefore, be some link of a logical rather than a causal sort between the 'means' and the 'end' if it is to be a process of learning. If anyone, for instance, is to learn to think mathematically or morally, the learning situations must include some kind of experiences of a mathematical or a moral sort. Learning may be aided by the temperature of the room, by constant repetition, by smiling at the learner or rewarding him. Some of these conditions of

learning may be of a causal type. But there must be some kind of logical link between the content to which the learner is introduced in the learning situation and that which is constitutive of his performance when he has learnt.

Because of this logical type of relationship between means and ends in education it is not appropriate to think of the values of an educational process as contained purely in the various attainments which are constitutive of being an educated person. For in most cases the logical relationship of means to ends is such that the values of the product are embryonically present in the learning process. Suppose, for instance, that children learn to think scientifically by being set simple problems to solve in chemistry and physics. Some of the values of scientific thinking — for instance being clear and precise, looking for evidence, checking results and not cooking them — are instantiated in the learning situation.[2] This would suggest that, from the point of view of value, there is little difference between the learning situation and that of the exercise of what has been learnt. This has led thinkers such as Dewey to claim that the values of living are no different from those of education. For both the learner and the liver exhibit the virtues of critical, open-ended, disciplined inquiry.

On the other hand there is the type of difference to which Aristotle drew attention in his paradox of moral education which is really the paradox of all education. This is that in order to develop the dispositions of a just man the individual has to perform acts that are just, but the acts which contribute to the formation of the dispositions of the just man are not conceived of in the same way as the acts which finally flow from his character, once he has become just. Similarly, doing science or reading poetry at school contribute to a person being educated. But later on, as an educated person, he may conceive of them very differently. He may do them because he is drawn to their underlying point or because he sees their relevance to some issue of belief or conduct. This makes the justification of values immanent in such activities very complicated. However, nothing yet has been said about the justification of any of the values of being educated.

2 Instrumental justifications of education

The most all-pervading type of justification for anything in our type of society is to look for its use either to the community or to the individual; for basically our society is geared to consumption. Even the work of the artist, for instance, is not always valued for the excellences which are intrinsic to it. Rather it is valued because it attracts more people to a public place, because it provides a soothing or restful atmosphere for people who are exposed to it, or because of the prestige of the artist which rubs off on to the body which commissions him. Music is piped into railway stations and air terminals to make people feel cheerful just as heat is piped through radiators to make them warm. Art and music can be thought of in this way irrespective of how the artists or musicians conceive of what they are doing. The same sort of thing can happen to education, though there are difficulties in thinking of education in this way if all its criteria are taken into account. To make this point I will consider its aspects separately.

(a) *Knowledge and understanding*. It can be argued cogently that the development of knowledge, skill, and understanding is in both the community's and the individual's interest because of other types of satisfaction which it promotes, and because of distinctive evils which it mitigates. Skills are an obvious case in point. Whatever their intrinsic value as forms of excellence the learning of them is obviously necessary for the survival of a community. Many of them also provide an individual with a living and hence with food, shelter, and a range of consumer satisfactions.

A strong instrumental case can also be made for the passing on of knowledge and understanding. Knowledge, in general, is essential to the survival of a civilized community in which processes of communication are very important. For 'knowledge' implies at least (i) that what is said or thought is true and (ii) that the individual has grounds for what he says or thinks. It is no accident that all civilized societies have such a concept. As far as (i) is concerned, most forms of communication would be impossible if people did not, in general, say what they thought was true. It is socially important, therefore, to have a special word to mark out communications drawing attention to what is true. (ii) The evidence condition is also socially very important because of the value of reliability and predictability in social life. Most of human behaviour depends on beliefs which are expressed and transmitted by means of language. If such beliefs were entirely based on guesses, on feelings which people had in their stomachs, or on various forms of divination, a predictable form of social life would be difficult to imagine. It is no accident, therefore, that civilized societies have the special word 'knowledge' which signals that the person who uses it has good grounds for what he says or thinks.

'Understanding' is equally important; for it suggests that a particular event can be explained in terms of a general principle or shown to fit into some kind of pattern or framework. This permits a higher degree of predictability because of the recourse to generality or to analogy. The context of predictability is thus widened. And, needless to say, the development of knowledge and understanding has an additional social benefit because it permits better control over and utilization of the natural world for human purposes as was emphasized by thinkers such as Bacon, Hobbes, and Marx. Hence the social value of highly specialized knowledge with the development of industrialism.

The development of understanding is particularly important in a modern industrialized society in which the skills required change rapidly. Industrialists do not demand that the schools should provide a lot of specialized technical training. They prefer to do this themselves or to arrange courses in technical colleges for their employees. If people just serve an apprenticeship in a specialized skill and if they are provided only with a body of knowledge which is necessary to the exercise of that skill under specific conditions, then they will tend to be resistant to change and will become redundant when there is no longer need for this particular skill. If, on the other hand, they have also some understanding in depth of what they are about, they will, at least, be more flexible in their approach and more ready to acquire new techniques. This applies also to social understanding, some degree of which is necessary for working with others; for, as Marx showed, changes in techniques bring with them changes in social organization. If a builder or a teacher is both limited in his understanding and rigid in his attitudes, he is not likely to be good at adapting to changes in organization brought about by changes in techniques.

(b) *Breadth of understanding.* The importance of social understanding suggests an instrumental type of argument for the other aspect of being educated which is incompatible with narrow specialization, namely that of 'breadth'. But what kind of case, in terms of providing services, can be made for typists, dentists, and shop stewards being aesthetically sensitive, and alive to their historical situation and religious predicament? A case can be made for such breadth of understanding as being an important aspect of political education in a democracy along the lines argued by Mrs White in her article on this subject.[3] It is, however, often said that such people make more efficient employees than those with a narrow training. But if this is true, which is questionable, it may not be due to the breadth of their understanding and sensitivity but to the fact that, in studying various subjects, they become practised in the generalizable techniques of filing papers and ideas, mastering and marshalling other people's arguments, of presenting alternatives clearly and weighing them up, of writing clearly and speaking articulately, and so on. Their academic training in the administration of ideas may prepare them for being administrators.

Of course it may be argued that educated people are of benefit to the professions and to industry because the breadth of their sensitivities helps to make their institutions more humane and civilized. But this is to abandon the instrumental form of argument in which qualities of mind are regarded purely as contributing to the efficiency of the service provided judged by some obvious criterion such as profit, number of patients cured, amount of food produced, and so on. As soon as industry or the professions come to be looked at not simply as providing profit, goods for consumption, or services to the public, but as being themselves constitutive of a desirable way of life, then the values associated with consumption begin to recede. And this introduces the third aspect of being educated.

(c) *Non-instrumental attitude.* It is difficult to make

explicit quite what is involved in this non-instrumental attitude. The key to it is that regard, respect, or love should be
shown for the intrinsic features of activities. This can be
exemplified in at least the following ways. First it involves
doing things for reasons that are reasons for doing this sort
of thing rather than for reasons that can be artificially tacked
on to almost anything that can be done. By that I mean that
most things can be done for profit, for approval, for reward,
to avoid punishment, for fame, for admiration. Such reasons
are essentially extrinsic, as distinct from intrinsic reasons
which are internal to the conception of the activity. If, for
instance, a teacher changes his methods because his pupils
seem too bored to learn, that is a reason intrinsic to the activity; for 'teaching' implies the intention to bring about
learning.

Second, if things are done for some end which is not extrinsic in this sense, the features of the means matter. If, for
instance, someone wants to get to another town or country
and is absolutely indifferent to the merits of different ways
of travelling, save in so far as he arrives quickly at his destina-
tion, then he has an instrumental attitude to travelling.

Third, well established activities such as gardening, teaching, and cooking have standards which are constitutive of
performing them well. These are usually related to the point
of the activity. If the individual cares about the point of the
activity he will therefore care about the standards which are
related to its point. If, for instance, he is committed to an
inquiry because he genuinely wants to find something out, he
will value clarity, will examine evidence carefully, and will
attempt to eliminate inconsistencies.

The ingenious could, no doubt, give arguments from the
outside in terms of benefits to consumers for the capacity
for doing and making things out of love for the job rather
than for some extrinsic reason. It could be claimed, for
instance, that bricklayers or doctors in fact render better
service to the public if they approach their tasks with this
attitude rather than with their minds on their pay packet
or someone else's satisfaction. But this is like the utilitarian
argument in favour of encouraging religious belief if it com-
forts the believer and ensures his social conformity. In both

93

cases the practice is looked at without any regard to its intrinsic nature. It is assessed from the outside purely in terms of its actual results, not at all in terms of how it is conceived by its participants. This, of course, is not an entirely irrelevant or immoral way of looking at a practice. But if it predominates a widespread and insidious type of corruption ensues. For the point of view of participants in a practice becomes of decreasing importance. They are regarded basically as vehicles for the promotion of public benefit, whose queer attitudes may sometimes promote this, though no thought of it ever enters their heads. This is the manipulator's attitude to other human beings, the 'hidden hand' in operation from the outside.

3 The incompleteness of instrumental justifications

All these arguments for education deriving from social benefit could also be put in terms of individual benefit with equal plausibility or lack of it. For it merely has to be pointed out that if certain types of knowledge and skill are socially beneficial, then it will be in the individual's interest to acquire some of them; for he has to earn a living and he will be likely to get prestige and reward for his possession of skills and knowledge that are socially demanded. He is afloat in the pool of relevantly trained manpower. There is also a lot of knowledge which will help him spend and consume more wisely — e.g. about types of food, house purchase, income tax, and so on. So the same kind of limited instrumental case can be made for education when it is looked at externally from the individual's point of view as when it is looked at from the point of view of social benefit. But there is an obvious incompleteness about these sorts of social justification, even if they are quite convincing — e.g. the justification for specialized knowledge. For what, in the end, constitutes social benefit? On what is the individual going to spend his wages? If approval is the lure, why should some things rather than others be approved of? What account is to be given of the states of affairs in relation to which other things are to be thought of as instrumental?

The answer of those whose thoughts veer towards

consumption is that social benefit is constituted by various forms of pleasure and satisfaction. This, however, is an unilluminating answer; for pleasure and satisfaction are not states of mind supervenient on doing things. Still less is happiness. They are inseparable from things that are done, whether this be swimming, eating a beef-steak, or listening to a symphony. And if it is said that such things are pleasures or done for the pleasure or satisfaction that they give, this is at least to suggest that they are done in a non-instrumental way. The reasons for doing them arise from the intrinsic features of the things done. So this is to repeat that they need no instrumental justification; they are indeed the sorts of things for the sake of which other things are done. It can then be asked why some pleasures rather than others are to be pursued. For many the pursuit of knowledge ranks as a pleasure. So this is no more in need of justification than any other form of pleasure — and no less.

The question, therefore, is whether knowledge and understanding have strong claims to be included as one of the goods which are *constitutive* of a worthwhile level of life and on what considerations their claims are based. This is a particularly pertinent question in the context of the value of education. For it was argued that the instrumental arguments for the breadth of knowledge of the educated man are not very obvious. Also it has been claimed that the educated person is one who is capable, to a certain extent, of a non-instrumental outlook. This would suggest that he does not think of his knowledge purely in terms of the uses to which he can put it. How then can it be justified?

4 Non-instrumental justifications of education

Questions about the intrinsic value of states of mind and of activities are often put by asking whether they are 'worth while'. This term is often used, of course, to raise questions of extrinsic value. If a man is asked whether gardening is worth while he may take it to be a question about its cash value. The term, too, is often used to draw attention to an individual's benefit, or lack of it, from something — e.g. 'It simply is not worth while for him to change his job just before he retires.' But even in its intrinsic uses it has ambiguities. (*a*) It can be used to indicate that an activity is likely to prove absorbing, to be an enjoyable way of passing the time. (*b*) Alternatively it can point to 'worth' that has little to do with absorption or enjoyment. Socrates obviously regarded questioning young men as being worth while; for it was an activity in which they came to grasp what was true, which, for him was a state of mind of ultimate value. But at times he may have found it a bit boring. Let us therefore explore the 'worthwhileness' of education in these two senses.

(a) *Absence of boredom*. An educated person is one who is possessed of a range of dispositions connected with knowledge and understanding. These will be revealed in what he says, in his emotional expressions, and in what he does. Of particular importance are the activities on which he spends time and the manner in which he engages in them. Activities can be more or less interesting, absorbing, or fascinating, depending on the dispositions and competences of the agent and the characteristics of the activity in question. Fishing, for instance, is more absorbing in one respect for a man who depends on fish for his meals or livelihood than for one who does it for sport; but in another respect the interest depends not so much on the urgency of the objective as on the skill there is in it. The more occasions there are for exercising skill in dealing with the unexpected, the more fascinating it becomes as an activity.

Some activities are absorbing because of their palpable and pleasurable point, such as eating, sexual activity, and fighting. But erected on this solid foundation of want is often an elaborate superstructure of rules and conventions which make it possible to indulge in these activities with more or less skill, sensitivity, and understanding. Such activities become 'civilized' when rules develop which protect those engaged in them from brutal efficiency in relation to the obvious end of the exercise. Eating could consist in getting as much food into the stomach in the quickest and most efficient way — like pigs at a trough. Civilization begins when conventions develop which protect others from the starkness of such 'natural' behaviour. The development of rules and conventions governing the manner in which these activities are pursued, because of the joys involved in mastery, generates an additional source of interest and pleasure.

To take part in activities of this civilized type requires considerable knowledge and understanding. The possession of it at least makes life less boring, as well as making possible levels of boredom beyond the ken of the uneducated. A case may be made, therefore, for the possession of knowledge in so far as it transforms activities by making them more complex and by altering the way in which they are conceived. This can take place in the pursuit of pleasures like those of the palate; it can also take place in spheres of duty which are sometimes regarded as boring. And in spheres like those of politics, or administration, which can be looked at both as pleasures and as duties, the degree of knowledge with which the activities are conducted makes a marked difference. For what there is in politics, administration, or business depends to a large extent on what a person conceives of himself as doing when he engages in them.

Another way in which knowledge can exert a transforming influence on conduct is in the sphere of planning — not just in the planning of means to ends within activities but in the avoidance of conflict between activities. This is where talk of happiness, integration, and the harmony of the soul has application. The question is not whether something should be indulged in *for the sake* of something else but whether indulging in some activity to a considerable extent is compatible with indulging in another which may be equally worth while. A man who wants to give equal expression to his passions for golf, gardening, and girls is going to have problems, unless he works out his priorities and imposes some sort of schedule on the use of his time. The case for the use of reason in this sphere of planning is not simply that by imposing coherence on activities conflict, and hence dissatisfaction, are avoided; it is also that the search for order and its implementation in life is itself an endless source of satisfaction. The development of knowledge is inseparable from classification and systematizing. In planning there is the added satisfaction of mastery, of imposing order and system on resistant material. Children begin to delight in this at the stage of concrete operations, and, when more abstract thought

97

develops, it is a potent source of delight. The love of order permeates Plato's account of reason and Freud regarded it as one of the main effective sources of civilization.

The mention of the pursuit of knowledge introduces another type of justification for knowledge and hence for education. For so far the case for knowledge in relation to the avoidance of boredom has been confined to its transforming influence on other activities. A strong case can be made for it, however, as providing a range of activities which are concerned with its development as an end in itself and which provide an endless source of interest and satisfaction in addition to that concerned with the love of order.

Philosophers from Plato onwards have made strong claims for the pursuit of knowledge as providing the most permanent source of satisfaction and absorption. They have claimed, not altogether convincingly, that the ends of most activities have certain obvious disadvantages when compared with the pursuit of truth. The ends of eating and sex, for instance, depend to a large extent on bodily conditions which are cyclic in character and which limit the time which can be spent on them; there are no such obvious limitations imposed on theoretical activities. Questions of scarcity of the object cannot arise either; for no one is prevented from pursuing truth if many others get absorbed in the same quest. There is no question either, as Spinoza argued so strongly, of the object perishing or passing away.

Theoretical activities could also be defended in respect of the unending opportunities for skill and discrimination which they provide. Most activities consist in bringing about the same state of affairs in a variety of ways under differing conditions. One dinner differs from another just as one game of bridge differs from another. But there is a static quality about them in that they both have either a natural or a conventional objective which can be attained in a limited number of ways. In science or history there is no such attainable objective. For truth is not an object that can be attained; it is an aegis under which there must always be progressive development. To discover something, to falsify the views of one's predecessors, necessarily opens up fresh things to be discovered, fresh hypotheses to be falsified. There must therefore necessarily be unending opportunities for fresh discrimination and judgment and for the development of further skills. An educated person, therefore, who keeps learning in a variety of forms of knowledge, will have a variety of absorbing pursuits to occupy him. The breadth of his interests will minimize the likelihood of boredom.

These arguments carry weight, but they are not entirely convincing. Even an educated person might claim that they are one-sided. In relation to the nature of the ends of activities he might argue that evanescence is essential to the attraction of some pursuits. What would wine-tasting or sexual activity be like if the culminating point was too permanent and prolonged? And is there not something to be said for excursions into the simple and brutish? Does not intensity of pleasure count as well as duration? In relation, too, to the arguments in terms of the open-endedness and progressive features of the pursuit of knowledge, it might well be said that the vision of life presented is altogether too exhausting. It smacks too much of John Dewey and the frontier mentality. It takes too little account of the conservative side of human nature, the enjoyment of routines, and the security to be found in the well-worn and the familiar.

(b) *The values of reason.* The major objection to these types of argument for the pursuit of knowledge, or for the transformation of other activities by the development of knowledge, is not to be found, however, within these dimensions or argument. It is rather to exclusive reliance on this form of argument. It is to the presupposition that, leaving aside straightforward moral arguments in terms of justice or the common good, science or wisdom in politics have to be defended purely hedonistically. This is not to say that arguments for education in terms of absorption and satisfaction are not important. Of course they are — especially with the increase in leisure time in modern society and the boring character of so many jobs. It is only to say that this is only one way of justifying education. To gain a fuller perspective we must turn to the other sense of 'worth while'.

In section 2(a) the connection between 'knowledge' and 'truth' was spelled out. To 'know' implies that what is said or thought is true and that the individual has grounds for what he says or thinks. The utilitarian case both for having a concept of knowledge and for the importance of knowledge in the life of the society and of the individual was briefly indicated. But being concerned about truth has another type of worth. It can be regarded as having a worth which is independent of its benefit. Indeed, the state of mind of one who is determined to find out what is true and who is not obviously deluded or mistaken about how things are can be regarded as an ultimate value which provides one of the criteria of benefit. This was the central point of Socrates's answer to Callicles in Plato's *Gorgias*. Someone who values truth in this way may find the constant effort to free his mind from prejudice and error painful; he may sometimes find it wearisome and boring; but it matters to him supremely, even if he falls short of the ideal which he accepts.

Three points must be briefly made to explain further this ideal. First no finality is assumed or sought for. It is appreciated that error is always possible. Value attaches as much to the attempt to eradicate error as it does to the state of not being in error. Second no positivistic view of truth is being assumed, which claims that true statements can only be made in the realms of empirical science, logic, and mathematics. Rather the term is being used widely to cover fields such as morals and understanding other people in which some kind of objectivity is possible, in which reasons can be given which count for or against a judgment. Third there is a group of virtues which are inseparable from any attempt to decide questions in this way. They are those of truth-telling and sincerity, freedom of thought, clarity, non-arbitrariness, impartiality, a sense of relevance, consistency, respect for evidence, and for people as the source of it — to mention the main ones. These must be accepted as virtues by anyone who is seriously concerned with answering questions by the use of reason.

How, then, is this concern for truth relevant to the attempt to justify knowledge and understanding? Surely because the activity of justification itself would be unintelligible without it. If a justification is sought for doing X rather than Y, then first X and Y have to be distinguished in some way. To distinguish them we have to rely on the forms of discrimination which are available, to locate them within some kind of conceptual scheme. For instance, if the choice is between going into medicine or going into business some understanding of these activities is a prerequisite. Understanding such activities is an open-ended business depending upon how they are conceived and how many aspects of them are explored. So an open-ended employment of various forms of understanding is necessary. And such probing must be conducted at least on the presupposition that obvious misconceptions of what is involved in these activities are to be removed. There is a presumption, in other words, that it is undesirable to believe what is false and desirable to believe what is true.

Second, if a reason is to be given for choosing *X* rather than *Y*, *X* has to be shown to have some feature which *Y* lacks which is relevant to its worth or desirability. If smoking in fact is a threat to health and chewing gum is not, these are relevant considerations, given the assumption that health is desirable. And this, in its turn, presupposes two types of knowledge, one about the effects of smoking as distinct from chewing gum, and the other about the desirability of health. Further questions can, of course, be raised about the desirability of health, which may lead to questions in moral philosophy about the existence and epistemological status of ultimate ends. But whatever the outcome of such explorations they too are part of the quest for further clarity and understanding. Maybe the inquirer will be chary of saying that what he ends up with is 'knowledge', but at least he may claim to have eliminated some errors and to have obtained more clarity and understanding of the issues involved. Arbitrary assertions will have been rejected, irrelevant considerations avoided, and generalizations queried for their evidential basis. These procedures, which are constitutive of the search for truth, are not those for which some individual might have a private preference; they are those which he must observe in rational discussion. This would be unintelligible as a public practice without value being ascribed at least to the elimination of muddle and error.

It might be admitted that there are links of this sort between justification and forms of knowledge in that to ask for reasons for believing or doing anything is to ask for what is only to be found in knowledge and understanding. But three sorts of difficulties might be raised about ascribing value to this concern for what is true. First, the value of justification itself might be queried. Second, it might be suggested that this does not establish the value of *breadth* of knowledge. Third, it might be argued that this only establishes the instrumental value of attempts to discover what is true. These three types of difficulty must be dealt with in turn.

(i) *The value of justification.* The difficulty about querying the value of justification is that any such query, if it is not frivolous, presupposes its value. For to discuss its value is immediately to embark upon reasons for or against it, which is itself a further example of justification. This is not, as might be thought, a purely *ad hominem* argument which might be produced to confound a reflective sceptic. For to give reasons why unreflective people should concern themselves more with what they do, think, and feel is to accept the very values that are at issue. No reason, therefore, can be given for justification without presupposing the values which are immanent in it as an activity.

It might be thought that this smacks of arbitrariness. But this is not so; for 'arbitrariness' is a complaint that only has application within a context where reasons can be given. To pick out the values presupposed by the search for reasons is to make explicit what gives point to the charge of arbitrariness. There is an important sense, too, in which anyone who denies the value of justification, not by making a case against it, which is to presuppose it, but by unreflectively relying on feelings in his stomach or on what other people say, is himself guilty of arbitrariness; for human life is a context in which the demands of reason are inescapable. Ultimately they cannot be satisfied by recourse to such methods. So anyone who relies on them is criticizable in the sense that he adopts procedures which are inappropriate to demands that are admitted, and must be admitted by anyone who takes part in human life.

To explain this point properly would require a treatise on man as a rational animal. All that can be here provided is a short sketch of the broad contours of the demand for justification that is immanent in human life. Human beings, like animals, have from the very start of their lives expectations of their environment, some of which are falsified. With the development of language these expectations come to be formulated and special words are used for the assessment of the content of these expectations and for how they are to be regarded in respect of their epistemological status. Words like 'true' and 'false' are used, for instance, to appraise the contents, and the term 'belief' for the attitude of mind that is appropriate to what is true. Perceiving and remembering are distinguished by their built-in truth claims from merely imagining. Knowledge is similarly distinguished from opinion. In learning we come up to standards of correctness as a result of past experience. Our language, which is riddled with such appraisals, bears witness to the claims of reason on our sensibility. It reflects our position as fallible creatures, beset by fears and wishes, in a world whose regularities have laboriously to be discovered.

The same sort of point can be made about human conduct. For human beings do not just veer towards goals like moths towards a light; they are not just programmed by an instinctive equipment. They conceive of ends, deliberate about them and about the means to them. They follow rules and revise and assess them. Assessment indeed has a toe-hold in every feature of this form of behaviour which, in this respect, is to be contrasted with that of a man who falls off a cliff or whose knee jerks when hit with a hammer. Words like 'right', 'good', and 'ought' reflect this constant scrutiny and monitoring of human actions.

Man is thus a creature who lives under the demands of reason. He can, of course, be unreasonable or irrational; but these terms are only intelligible as fallings short in respect of reason. An unreasonable man has reasons, but bad ones; an irrational man acts or holds beliefs in the face of reasons. But how does it help the argument to show that human life is only intelligible on the assumption that the demands of reason are admitted, and woven into the fabric of human life? It helps because it makes plain that the demands of reason are not just an option available to the reflective. Any man who emerges from infancy tries to perceive, to remember, to infer, to learn, and to regulate his wants. If he is to do this he must have recourse to some procedure of assessment. For how else could he determine what to believe or do? In their early years all human beings are initiated into human life by their elders and rely for a long time on procedures connected with authority and custom. They believe what they are told and do what others do and expect of them. Many manage most of their lives by reliance on such procedures. This fact, however, is a reflection of human psychology rather than of the logic of the situation; for ultimately such procedures are inappropriate to the demand that they are meant to serve. For belief is the attitude which is appropriate to what is true, and no statement is true just because an individual or a group proclaims it. For the person whose word is believed has himself to have some procedure for determining what is true. In the end there must be procedures which depend not just on going on what somebody else says but on looking at the reasons which are relevant to the truth of the statement. The truth of a lot of statements depends upon the evidence of the senses; and all men have sense-organs. Similarly reasons for action are connected with human wants; and all men have wants. There may be good reasons, in certain spheres of life, for reliance on authorities; but such authorities, logically speaking, can only be regarded as provisional. They cannot be regarded as the ultimate source of what is true, right, and good. This goes against the logic of the situation.

Thus those who rely permanently and perpetually on custom or authority are criticizable because they are relying on procedures of assessment which are not ultimately appropriate to the nature of belief and conduct. To say, therefore, that men ought to rely more on their reason, that they ought to be more concerned with first-hand justification, is to claim that they are systematically falling down on a job on which they are already engaged. It is not to commit some version of the naturalistic fallacy by basing a demand for a type of life on features of human life which make it distinctively human. For this would be to repeat the errors of the old Greek doctrine of function. Rather it is to say that human life already bears witness to the demands of reason. Without some acceptance by men of such demands their life would be unintelligible. But given the acceptance of such demands they are proceeding in a way which is inappropriate to satisfying them. Concern for truth is written into human life. There are procedures which are ultimately inappropriate for giving expression to this concern.

This is not to say, of course, that there are not *other* features of life which are valuable — love for others, for instance. It is not even to say that other such concerns may not be more valuable. It is only to say that at least some attempt must be made to satisfy the admitted demands that reason makes upon human life. If, for instance, someone is loved under descriptions which are manifestly false, this is a fault. If, too, a person is deluded in thinking that he loves someone — if, for instance, he mistakes love of being loved for loving someone — this too is a criticism.

This argument, which bases the case for the development of knowledge and understanding on its connection with justification, does not make a case for the pursuit of any kind of knowledge. It only points to the importance of knowledge that is relevant to the assessment of belief, conduct, and feeling. It does not show, for instance, that there is value in amassing a vast store of information, in learning by heart every tenth name in a telephone directory. And this accords well with the account of the sort of knowledge that was ascribed to an educated person. For to be educated is to have one's view of the world transformed by the development and systematization of conceptual schemes. It is to be disposed to ask the reason why of things. It is not to have a store of what Whitehead called 'inert ideas'.

(ii) *The case for breadth*. It might still be claimed, however, that this type of argument only shows the value of some sort of knowledge; it does not establish the value of the breadth of understanding characteristic of the educated man. A man might just look for grounds of a certain sort of beliefs — e.g. empirical grounds. He might only value philosophy.

The case for breadth derives from the original link that was claimed between justification and forms of knowledge. For if a choice has to be made between alternatives these have both to be sampled in some way and discriminated in some way. It is not always possible to do the former but the latter must be done for this to rank as a choice. The description of possible activities open to anyone and hence the discussion of their value is not a matter of mere observation. For they depend, in part, on how they are conceived, and this is very varied. If the choice is, for instance, between an activity like cooking or one like art or science, what is going to be emphasized as characterizing these activities? Many such activities — chess, for instance, or mathematics — are difficult to understand without a period of initiation. But they cannot simply be engaged in; they have to be viewed in a certain way. And this will depend upon the forms of understanding that are available and the extent to which the individual has been initiated into them. It would be unreasonable, therefore, to deprive anyone of access in an arbitrary way to forms of understanding which might throw light on alternatives open to him. This is the basic argument for breadth in education.

In the educational situation we have positively to put others in the way of such forms of understanding which may aid their assessment of options open to them. It is of great importance in a society such as ours in which there are many life-styles open to individuals and in which they are encouraged to choose between them, and to make something of themselves. But this value accorded to autonomy, which demands criticism of what is handed on and some first-hand assessment of it, would be unintelligible without the values immanent in justification. Indeed it is largely an implementation of them. For it demands not only critical reflection on rules and activities, with the search for grounds that this involves, but also a genuineness which is connected with the rejection of second-hand considerations. By that I mean that a conventionally minded person goes on what others say. If he has reasons for doing things these are connected with the approval which he will get if he does them and the disapproval if he does not. These are reasons of a sort but are artifically related to what is done. They are reasons for doing a whole variety of things, not this thing in particular. If, for instance, people refrain from smoking because they are disapproved of if they do, this is not connected with smoking in the way in which the probability of lung cancer is connected. As Hume put this point in the context of morality: 'no action

106

can be virtuous or morally good unless there be in human nature some motive to produce it distinct from the sense of its morality'. The same sort of point can be made about other forms of judgment — e.g. aesthetic, scientific, religious. So if the individual is to be helped to discriminate between possibilities open to him in an authentic, as distinct from a second-hand way, he has to be initiated into the different forms of reasoning which employ different criteria for the relevance of reasons.

A corollary of this type of argument for breadth of understanding would be that some forms of knowledge are of more value from the point of view of a 'liberal education' than others, namely those which have a more far-reaching influence on conceptual schemes and forms of understanding. There are forms of understanding such as science, philosophy, literature, and history which have a far-ranging cognitive content. This is one feature which distinguishes them from 'knowing how' and the sort of knowledge that people have who are adepts at games and at practical skills. There is a limited amount to know about riding bicycles, swimming, or golf. Furthermore, what is known sheds little light on much else.

Science, history, literary appreciation, and philosophy, on the other hand, have a far-ranging cognitive content which gives them a value denied to other more circumscribed activities. They consist largely in the explanation, assessment, and illumination of the different facets of life. They can thus insensibly change a man's view of the world. The point, then, about activities such as science, philosophy, and history is that they need not, like games, be isolated and confined to set times and places. A person who has pursued them systematically can develop conceptual schemes and forms of appraisal which transform everything else that he does.

(iii) *An instrumental type of argument?* But, it might be said, this shows only the *instrumental* value of breadth of understanding and imagination. It does not show that a variety of forms of knowledge should be pursued for any other reason, particularly if they are rather boring. This argument also shows the great importance of physical education. For without a fit body a man's attempts to answer the question 'Why do this rather than that?' might be sluggish or slovenly. So it provides, it seems, a transcendental deduction of the principle of physical fitness! The seeming correctness of such a deduction, if the empirical connection were to be shown, does not establish that physical exercise has any value except of an instrumental sort.

There is, however, a confusion in this comparison between physical exercise and the pursuit of knowledge in their relations to justification; for the former is suggested as an empirically necessary condition and hence is properly regarded as instrumental, whereas the latter is connected by logical relationships such as those of 'relevance', 'providing evidence', 'illuminating', and 'explaining'. Indeed the latter is in an educational type of relationship to justification in that it suggests avenues of learning which are relevant to choice, and this is not properly conceived of as an instrumental relationship, as was argued in section 1(d). In engaging in the activity of justification the individual is envisaged as exploring the possibilities open to him by developing the ways of discriminating between them that are available to him — i.e. through the different forms of understanding such as science, history, literature, which the human race has laboriously developed. This process of learning is logically, not causally related, to the questioning situation. He will be articulating, with increasing understanding and imagination, aspects of the situation in which he is placed, and in pursuing various differentiated forms of inquiry he will be instantiating, on a wider scale, the very values which are present in his original situation — e.g. respect for facts and evidence, precision, clarity, rejection of arbitrariness, consistency, and the general determination to get to the bottom of things. If, for instance, he considers one of the possibilities open to him as desirable he must, as has already been argued, view this under a certain description. The question then arises whether this description is really applicable and whether there is any other way of looking at this possibility which might be relevant. The ethical question immediately articulates itself into other sorts of questions. The values of reason, such as those of consistency, relevance, and clarity, inherent in such educational explorations, are the values of the starting-point 'writ large'.

It is important to stress the values of reason which are immanent in such attempts to discriminate alternatives with more clarity and precision rather than the 'means—end' type of link between questioning and forms of knowledge that can often be both logical, and of the 'means—end' type, as in the case of the relationship between learning to read and reading George Eliot, previously explained (see n. 2). Socrates, it seems, gave up his pursuit of knowledge in the physical sciences in favour of devotion to ethics and psychology. It could be argued that, leaving aside *other* questions to do with what he found absorbing, he could well have thought that he ought to study psychological questions deeply only because of their logical links with ethical questions. He had reason to engage in such a disinterested inquiry but did not value this form of knowledge 'for its own sake'. But this is to misconceive the way in which the value of concern for truth enters into both answering justificatory questions *and* into asking them. The point is that value is located in the procedures necessary to explicate what is meant by *justification*. In other words the value is not in the acquisition of knowledge *per se* but in the demands of reason inherent both in answering questions of this sort and in asking them. Evidence should be produced, questions should be clearly put, alternatives should be set out in a clear and informed way, inconsistencies and contradictions in argument should be avoided, relevant considerations should be explored, and arbitrariness avoided. These monitoring and warranting types of relationships, which are characteristic of the use of reason, are not instrumental types of relationship. They are articulations of the ideal implicit in thought and action. We are drawn towards this ideal by what I have elsewhere called the 'rational passions'.[4] And this ideal may draw us towards types of inquiry which we do not find particularly absorbing in their own right.

To put this point in another way: much has been said in this section about the 'concern for truth' and 'the demands of reason'. The value picked out by these expressions is not to be thought of as a kind of consumer value which bestows importance on the accumulation of countless true propositions. Devotion to the pursuit of knowledge, in this sense, may also be fascinating, and a case can be made for it in terms of the first sense of 'worth while'. But that type of argument is not now being used either. Value rather is being ascribed to the quality of knowledge rather than to its amount or to its capacity to mitigate boredom. It is being claimed that what is valuable is inherent in the demand that what is done, thought, or felt should be rationally scrutinized.

It will not do to suggest that this concern for truth is instrumentally valuable just because people need to know in order to satisfy their wants, including their desire for knowledge itself, unless 'want' is used in a very general sense which makes it a conceptual truth that anything which people can value must be, in some sense, what they want. For, first, to want is always to want under some description that involves belief; hence wants can be more or less examined. Second, one of the most perplexing questions of conduct is whether, in any ordinary sense of 'want', people ought to do what they want to do. Third, the very notion of 'instrumentality' presupposes the demand of reason. For, as Kant put it, taking a means to an end presupposes the axiom of reason that to will the end is to will the means. Thus the demands of reason are presupposed in the form of thought which might lead us to think of its value as being instrumental.

On the other hand the demand for truth is not an absolute demand in the sense that it can never be over-ridden. It sometimes can be, if, in some situation, some other value is more pressing. In general, for instance, it is undesirable that people should ignore facts about themselves or about others which are relevant to what they should do. But on a particular occasion, when someone's suffering is manifestly at stake for instance, it might be argued that it is just as well for a person not to be too persistent in his demand for truth, if satisfying this demand would occasion great suffering. The values of reason are only one type of value. As has been argued from the start, there are other values, e.g. love for others, the avoidance of suffering. But situations like this, in which there is a conflict of values, do not affect the general status of the concern for truth. As E. M. Forster put it: 'Yes, for we fight for more than Love or Pleasure: there is Truth. Truth counts. Truth does Count.'[5]

110

This type of argument for the value of knowledge helps to explain the value inherent in being educated, not only of breadth of knowledge, as previously explained, but also of what was called 'cognitive perspective'. What was suggested is that an educated person is not one who has his mind composed of *disconnected* items of knowledge. What he knows and understands should be seen to be interrelated in terms of consistency, relevance, evidence, implication, and other such rational connections. If his knowledge is linked together in this way it is 'integrated' in one sense of the term. It may well be, too, that certain studies such as philosophy, which explicitly examines grounds for different types of knowledge and their interrelationship, and literature, which imaginatively depicts people in situations in which they have to make complex judgments and respond emotionally to perplexing situations, contribute to the development of this cognitive perspective.

Those who favour certain educational methods might argue that the exploration of literature, of history, and of philosophy should not begin until children begin to be troubled or curious about various aspects of the human condition. And certainly, if inquiries and explorations move outwards from a centre of puzzlement and concern, they are more likely to be genuine and to instantiate the values immanent in justification in a first-hand way. Others, however, might argue that one way of generating such concern and puzzlement in people is to initiate them into our human heritage. This kind of imaginative situation may be necessary to make people more alive to their position in the world as believers and choosers. But there is the danger of the second-hand in this approach. There is also the possibility that individuals may fail to connect, to transfer values learnt in a specialized context to wider contexts. A person, for instance, may be ruthless in demanding evidence for assumptions when learning history or social science. But he may not show the same ruthlessness when having to make up his mind about policies presented to him by politicians. This raises questions which are, in part, empirical about transfer of learning. But it does not, I think, affect the basic point about the non-instrumental features of the relationship between justification,

111

and the forms of understanding which contribute to it.

In a purely philosophical context it might be said, then, that the demand for justification presupposes the acceptance of the values implicit in it. In an educational context, however, children must be initiated somehow into those forms of understanding which are of particular relevance to justification. It is, of course, no accident that there should be these two ways of explicating this relationship. For processes of education are processes by means of which people come to know and to understand. These are implementations, through time, by means of learning, of the values and procedures implicit in justification. Education, properly understood, is the attempt to actualize the ideal implicit in Socrates' saying that the unexamined life is not worth living.

5   The non-instrumental attitude

An educated person, it was argued, is characterized not just by his abiding concern for knowledge and understanding but also by the capacity to adopt, to a certain extent, a non-instrumental attitude to activities. How can this attitude be justified? This is not difficult; for the justification of it is implicit in what has already been said. It is presupposed by the determination to search for justification. Anyone who asks the question about his life 'Why do this rather than that?' has already reached the stage at which he sees that instrumental justifications must reach a stopping place in activities that must be regarded as providing end-points for such justifications. To ask of his pattern of life 'What is the point of it all?' is to ask for features internal to it which constitutes reasons for pursuing it. A stage has been reached at which the ordinary use of 'point' has no application — unless, that is, the same types of question are transferred to an afterlife or to the life of future generations. So a person who asks this type of question seriously demonstrates that he is not a stranger to this attitude. To what extent it will in fact transform his way of going about particular activities within his life cannot be inferred from this capacity for reflection. It is, to a certain extent, an empirical question — but not entirely empirical, because of the logical connection between the general capacity to reflect and particular instantiations of it.

In so far, however, as he values knowledge and understanding he values one very important ingredient in the non-instrumental attitude; for this attitude requires attention to the actual features of that with which he is confronted, as distinct from tunnel vision determined by his own wants. He is concerned about what is 'out there'. Even at the crudest level a person who *just* regards a piece of fish as a way of satisfying his hunger, or a glass of wine as a way of satisfying his thirst, ignores a range of features. He fails to discriminate the variety of tastes. Conversely he will think nothing of using a beautiful glass to house his tooth-brush — unless, of course, he thinks that it is worth a lot of money and that he might break it. In sexual activity, too, he will regard a woman as a necessary object for satisfying his lust; he will be indifferent to her idiosyncrasies and point of view as a person. He will only listen to people in so far as they share his purposes or provide, by their remarks, springboards for his own self-display. His interest in people and things is limited to the use he can make of them. He lacks interest in and concern for what is 'out there'.

A person, on the other hand, who presses the question 'Why do this rather than that?' already accepts the limitations of his egocentric vision. He is not satisfied with a life geared to unexamined wants. He wonders whether some of the things that he wants are really worth wanting or whether he really wants them. He wonders about the relevance of his wants. In attempting to find out what is the case he may reveal features of situations that in no way serve his wants and which indeed may run counter to them. An unreflective businessman, for instance, might visit an undeveloped country with a view to setting up a factory. But, on going into all the details of what this would involve, he might become more and more aware of the disruption of a way of life that is entailed. He might 'not want to know' or he might begin to question the whole enterprise. And if he began to question this particular feature of business life he might begin to query the way of life more generally.

Another aspect of the instrumental attitude is the view of time that goes with it. For the instrumentally minded good lies always in future consumption. The present has to be hurried through for the sake of what lies ahead. It is not to be dwelt in and its aspects explored. To a person who uses his reason this attitude is just as unreasonable as the opposed cult of instancy. For, as Sidgwick put it, to a rational person, 'Hereafter as such is to be regarded neither more nor less than now.'[6] Reasons have to be given for instant or delayed gratification other than temporal position — e.g. 'If you wait you won't be able to have it at all' or 'If you wait there will be more of it.' The important thing for a man is to connect, to grasp the features of objects and situations and the relationships which structure his life. It is not, therefore, the fact that the pleasure of smoking is to be had now or in five minutes that matters; it is rather how it is to be conceived and its relation to other things in life. Can smoking, like sexual activity, be conceived of not simply as a physical pleasure, but also as an expression of love? Can it be done with skill and grace like dancing? And are its relationships to other human activities anything other than detrimental?

To ascribe a non-instrumental attitude to a person is not, of course, to lay down that he will indulge in some activities rather than others. It is only to indicate the way in which he will go about activities and conceive them. He will not always do things for the sake of some extrinsic end. He will, first of all, enjoy performing well according to the standards required. He will have an attitude of care in other words. But this care will be related to the point of the activity. He will feel humility towards the givenness of the features of the activity, towards the impersonal demands of its standards. And he will have a sense of its connection with other things in life, a wary consciousness of the past and the future and of the place of what is being done in the passage through the present. Indeed, as Spinoza put it, he should be capable of viewing what he does 'under a certain aspect of eternity'.

6 Concluding problem

There is a major outstanding problem to which this approach to justification gives rise. Two types of value have been distinguished, which underpin the life of an educated person, leaving aside moral values such as justice, and the minimization of suffering, which structure the interpersonal realm of conduct. These are (i) values relevant to the avoidance of boredom, in relation to which the pursuit of knowledge was accorded a high place, and (ii) values implicit in the demands of reason which give rise to virtues such as humility, hatred of arbitrariness, consistency, clarity, and so on. If a reasonable person examines his beliefs or conduct these virtues govern his conduct of the inquiry; but he does not necessarily find this kind of examination enjoyable or absorbing.

Now, for reasons that were explained in Section 1(d), when dealing with processes of education, a person can only *become* educated if he pursues theoretical activities such as science and literature and/or practical activities which require a fair degree of understanding; but why, having become educated, should he devote himself much to activities of this sort? Why should he choose to spend much of his time in reading, taking part in discussions, or in demanding practical activities such as engineering? On occasions, of course, in acknowledgment of the demands of reason, he may feel obliged to enlighten himself on some issue, to seek information which is relevant to his beliefs and action. And while so doing he submits to the standards of such a disinterested pursuit. But why should he seek out *any* such pursuits? To take a parallel in the moral sphere: why should a person who accepts the principle of justice, and who acknowledges its demands on his life by relevant actions and inquiries when occasions arise, pursue the promotion of justice as an *activity* — e.g. by working as a judge or as a social reformer? Similarly, in this sphere of worthwhile pursuits, why should not an educated man settle for an undemanding job which allows him plenty of time for playing golf which is the one activity which he really enjoys apart from eating, sun-bathing, and occasionally making love to his wife? He is, of course, capable of seeing point in a more Dewey type of life of expanding experience and understanding. He is not a philistine; neither is he particularly instrumental in his outlook. He just loves his game of golf more than any of the more intellectually taxing types of pursuits. Golf is to him what he presumes science is to the other fellow.

115

Could the answer be connected with the fact, already pointed out, that the use of reason itself exemplifies the two
types of value? On the one hand is the absorption springing
from curiosity and from the love of order, etc. Human beings,
it might be said, 'naturally' find discrepancies between what
they expect and what they experience intolerable. This is
what leads them to learn according to cognitive theories of
motivation stemming from Piaget. On the other hand there
are the normative demands connected with the use of reason.
Inconsistencies and confusions in thought ought to be removed; evidence ought to be sought for and arbitrariness
avoided. Is it conceivable that the latter type of value could
be accepted by a person who was unmoved by curiosity and
by the desire to sort things out? Is this not like saying, in
the moral sphere, that respect for persons, as a moral attitude,
could exist without some natural sympathy for them?

There may well be some relationships, which are not purely
contingent, between the 'natural' and the normative aspects
of the use of reason, which may parallel those between sympathy and respect, but it would require another paper to
elucidate them. The doubt, as far as this paper goes, is
whether such connections need be strong enough to carry
the required weight. It might be shown that acceptance of
the demands of reason presupposes certain 'natural' passions
such as curiosity and the love of order, but would it show
enough to make it necessarily the case that an educated
person must not only proceed in a rational way with regard
to his beliefs and conduct but must also adopt some pursuits
for their own sake which provide ample scope for curiosity
or which are taxing in relation to the level of understanding that they require? Does not Dewey's educational method,
which requires that learning should always be harnessed to
spontaneous interest and curiosity, seem appropriate because
so many people emerge from school and university with some
degree of sophistication and capacity for rational reflection,
but with a singular lack of enthusiasm either for further
theoretical pursuits or for practical activities that make fre-
quent and open-ended demands on their understanding?
Could not his methods be seen as an attempt to close the
gap between the two types of value? And does not this

suggest that, as closing this gap depends upon empirical conditions underlying methods of learning, the connection in question is an empirical connection? Indeed, is not one of the main tasks of the educator the devising of procedures which are likely to minimize this type of gap?

This sounds plausible but a nagging doubt remains. The problem can be summarized as follows:

(i) There are activities such as science, engineering, the study of literature, etc., by engaging in which a person becomes an educated person — one who has breadth and depth of understanding and who is prepared to examine his beliefs and conduct.

(ii) As an educated person he may, later on, see reason to pursue such activities on occasions, if he sees their relevance to some issue of belief and conduct, though he may not find them particularly absorbing. Such exercises will be manifestations of his acceptance of the demands of reason.

(iii) But, as an educated person, he will do *some* things for their own sake. Whatever he does will be, to a certain extent, transformed by his level of understanding, but will he necessarily pursue, for their own sake, some activities of the sort that he pursues or has pursued in contexts (i) and (ii), which make demands on his understanding? Is it intelligible that he should both be educated and find *all* such activities too frustrating or boring to pursue for their own sake? Would such a man be any more intelligible than Kant's moral being who is virtuous only out of respect for the law? Socrates may have sometimes regarded his pursuit of truth with others as a boring duty, though we know that he did not always find it so. But does it not seem inconceivable that he could *always* have found it boring? And is this *simply* because of the empirical fact that he spent a lot of time that way?

Notes

My thanks are due to colleagues and friends who helped me by their criticism of early versions of this paper, especially Paul Hirst and A. Phillips Griffiths.
1 R. S Peters, 'Education and the Educated Man', *Proceedings of the Philosophy of Education Society of Great Britain*, vol. 4, January 1970.

2 In other cases, however, the logical relationship of the learning process to the product is that of being a necessary preliminary rather than a full-blooded instantiation. Reading, for instance, is often taught as a kind of discrimination skill. Practising such discriminations may be thought of as instantiating little that is valuable. It is valuable only as a necessary preliminary to reading poetry with sensitivity and expression, or to reading George Eliot's novels.

3 See P. A. White, 'Education, Democracy, and the Public Interest', in R. S. Peters (ed.), *The Philosophy of Education*, Oxford University Press, 1973.

4 See R. S. Peters, 'Reason and Passion', in G. Vezey (ed.), *The Proper Study*, Royal Institute of Philosophy, London, Macmillan, 1971.

5 E. M. Forster, *A Room with a View*, Harmondsworth, Penguin, 1955, p. 218.

6 H. Sidgwick, *The Methods of Ethics*, Papermac edn, London, Macmillan, 1962, p. 381.

Was Plato nearly right about education? 6

Introduction

In order to indicate the thrust of the title and of this essay I will tell a story, which, I hope, will not shock too many sensibilities. There was a man who went to a marriage bureau to meet the secretary who was trying to fix him up. After a bit of a discussion the secretary said 'Oh, I've got just the girl for you in my file. She comes from a similar background, and is about the same age, and height; her interests are very similar too. There's just one thing about her, though, which might make you pause — she's just a teeny weeny little bit pregnant!' That is really what I feel about Plato. There is just one little thing which is a bit daunting, if its implications are examined.

To develop this theme I propose to divide my talk into three main sections. First of all I shall give an exposition of Plato's proposals about education in some sort of logical order; for one of the most fascinating things about Plato's educational proposals is their logical structure. Second, I shall do what it seems to be important to do with any philosopher, namely to state where I think he was right. Then, third, I shall pass to the little point which seems to me, in its implications, to constitute a major objection to the whole brilliant conception.

In expounding Plato, there is, of course, the problem of historical relativism. By that I do not mean just the details, such as whether children went to school or not, but the whole problem of interpreting in our conceptual system what some of his major notions meant to him, e.g. 'reason', 'order', 'justice'. This presents problems if one gets down to such concepts in detail. Nevertheless, I am going to assume that many of his major ideas can be understood by us, more or less, in the same sort of way as he understood them, but I know this is a questionable assumption. What I want to argue is that Plato was right in seeing education to be centrally concerned with the development of reason and that, in the main, he had a very acceptable conception of reason — but there is just one major aspect of his conception of reason which is absolutely non-acceptable. That is going to prove to be the crucial objection to his system.

1 The logical structure of Plato's educational proposals

Let us look, first of all, at the structure of his educational proposals. What is so attractive about them is their lack of arbitrariness. They follow, quite logically, from a combination of value judgments and assumptions about human nature. In this way they are exemplary in structure because he had a worked-out theory of knowledge, an ethical theory and a theory of human nature. No educational theory can be viable without having these three major components, because, in my view, education is concerned with the development of states of mind involving understanding and knowledge, which are thought valuable, and which have to be attained by processes of learning, which are linked with a view of human nature, and how it develops.

(i) Value-judgments

Let us first of all, then, consider the value judgments which underlie Plato's whole system. They are one of two types. One relates to the individual, and the other to the political system and the role of the individual in it. In relation to the individual he maintained quite uncompromisingly that the life of reason is the best life possible. This was to be understood in three ways: first of all, he meant by this that the theoretical life (and this meant for him the study of philosophy, mathematics and harmonics) was the best sort of life. This bore witness to the Pythagorean influence on Plato. By coming to understand the underlying structure of the world in such studies the soul becomes one with the Forms. The mind begins to mirror or represent in itself reality, which has a kind of purging influence on the soul.

120

Second, there was the more practical aspect of reason, Socrates' 'care of the soul' which was later developed by Aristotle more explicitly. This was exhibited in self-knowledge and self-control. Third, supporting both aspects of reason, both theoretical and practical, was his account of Eros, or desire. The contrast between reason and passion, on Plato's view, was absurd. He distinguished levels of passion; there was a level of passion which accompanied the life of reason which was distinct from that accompanying the life of the political man, of the warrior, and so on. In other words the use of reason is a passionate business whether you are in pursuit of the Forms or whether you are developing some kind of order in yourself.

These, then, were the basic valuative assumptions about the best life for the individual. Second, there were his valuative assumptions about the state, which are more familiar, and which are to be understood, I think, in terms of the rise of professionalism at the time, represented by Isocrates and others, and evident in the dislike of people like Plato and Isocrates for the 'happy versatility' of Pericles' funeral speech. Plato had a supreme contempt for the amateur. He thought that any art has an underlying theory and that anyone who is a professional understands the theory and knows how to apply it. That was one background influence. Then there was the purely historical contingency of the divorce of knowledge from power since the death of Pericles and the rise of demagogues like Cleon. Further, as the Peloponnesian War progressed, there was the upsurge of self-seeking individualism exemplified in the Melian expedition and above all, in Plato's mind, in the career of Alcibiades which seemed to him to personify these sorts of tendencies. And finally, accompanying this, as exhibited in the works of Euripides especially, was the subjectivism, and scepticism, of the young.

Now, given this sort of background, Plato's uncompromising view was that ruling is a professional business and that there should be in the ruler a combination of authority and wisdom; that the wise should rule, and that the best state is the state ruled by those who are the best men. These are the men, who in their souls, display a passion for reason and understanding and who are able to apply this to their own behaviour and conduct.

121

I have no intention of going over Plato's arguments for these value judgments, which have been heavily criticised by people like Popper and Crossman. At least they are interesting. Whether they are valid is another question. All I have done is to make explicit what his value judgments are and to put them into some kind of context. I am leaving on one side the question of the validity of his attempt to justify them. So, given these value judgments about the type of men that are best, the problem of education is to produce people in whom reason is properly developed, who care about the objects of the theoretical life, who are not side-tracked by subjectivism, who know fully what they want, and who have the strength of character to carry it through. If you like, Plato's ideal was a combination of the Spartan and Athenian virtues.

(ii) Assumptions about human nature

Given these value judgments, if you are going to have an educational system, there is the problem of bringing these people into being. So certain assumptions have to be made about human nature. In Plato these assumptions can be divided into three types. First of all, there is the assumption about the raw material with which the teacher has to work. Plato, I think, was the first systematic environmentalist; he thought that human nature is more or less infinitely malleable. For him Alcibiades was the lesson for all time. Here was a man born with a certain potential, obviously of very high intelligence; but because of his early upbringing even Socrates could do little with him when he became an adolescent. A pattern had been set in his childhood which was almost irreversible. I think that Plato was also what is often now called a perfectibilist, in that he thought that if you can get men in their early childhood, then, given their potential, and given the correct form of social influences, you can produce people like Gandhi or Sir Stafford Cripps or whatever might be the modern parallel for a philosopher-king. It is a matter of the sort of training which you give them. That was his first assumption about the raw material with which the educator is working.

The second one, of course, was that this human potential is unevenly distributed — something that people seem to get very hot under the collar about nowadays in the Jensen controversy. Plato was particularly interested in the differences between people in regard to their intelligence and their social sense — their capacity to co-operate for the common good. He thought that there were marked differences in these particular potentialities. So much then for Plato's assumptions about the raw material with which the educator is working.

The second sorts of assumption are about stages of development. They are now very familiar to us because of the work of Piaget, much of which was anticipated by Plato; for if you look at Plato's account of the stages of development, they are very Piagetian. First of all there is the Freudian level in which Piaget is not much interested. Freud argued that a small infant does not make the distinction between true and false. He has no concept of cause and effect; he does not understand the world in terms of material objects. In other words, he has not grasped the categories which enable us to distinguish what is real from what is imaginary. Plato said just this, that the small child lives in what he called the stage of εἰκασία, a sort of guess-work or conjecture; he has not got a reality principle or conception of objects or causality. He then gets to the stage of what Plato called δόξα which Piaget calls concrete operations. The world now consists of hard, solid objects which have palpable properties which can be perceived through the various senses. Then, finally, there is the stage of formal operations which actually Plato divided into two. He distinguished within formal operations between ἐπιστήμη and νοῦς; between the grasp of particular forms, and the kind of synoptic vision of how they all fit together, and how particular forms can be linked with the Supreme Form, the Form of the Good. Now, as we know, these stages of development in Plato were not worked out by sitting children down and asking them questions. There is a sense in which we know it already; for the stages of development form some kind of logical progression. The problem is to make it explicit and to convince people that what is manifestly true *is* true. Piaget, in my view, does it by doing what are meant to be experiments but which manifestly are not.

Plato did it by telling stories about the Line and Cave, which are a very graphic or dramatic way of making just these points about cognitive development.

Third, under his assumptions about human nature, come the ways in which people can be influenced in their development. And I think he has at least four suggestions here as to what is important in the way of special influences. First of all, there is the crucial role of what we now call identification or imitation; hence Plato's concern about the example of heroes and the stories of the Gods which were to be found in Homer, and his insistence on censorship. The example of teachers is also crucial. Second, there is the *indirect* influence of the environment, the influence of beautiful places and beautiful objects on the individual. Third he draws attention to the importance of play in learning. He talks very strongly about both the indignity and the inefficiency of compelling children to learn things that they do not want to know at that stage. (He says this particularly in the context of learning mathematics.) If children can learn things in a context where they enjoy doing what they are learning, especially while at play, then they are more likely to learn it. Finally, at the stage of reason proper, there is the importance of question and answer, of dialectic as a method of learning.

(iii) Consequent educational proposals

So much, then, for the assumptions about human nature. His educational proposals were generated by putting together the value judgments about the type of individuals to be produced with these assumptions about human nature. Whatever is done in education, for Plato, is a way of either developing in the individual the understanding and love of principles, and the passion for order and symmetry, or of helping the individual to use his reason to impose some harmony on his desires. This is the 'integration of the personality', or whatever you want to call it in modern jargon. In Plato's view gradually the order without is reflected in the order within the individual self. This was a notion which was used in a much more mystical way by Froebel in his writings.

How, then, is this aim of education to be achieved? The

guiding rule is that the way in which children are made sensitive to the order in the world, and hence to reproduce this in their own soul, must be appropriate to the stage at which they are. All Plato's educational proposals were therefore designed to sensitize individuals to form and order in the way which is practicable at the stage at which they are. So a start is to be made with the stories of gods and heroes, because, at the early stage of εἰκασία, when children cannot distinguish between what is real and imaginary, it does not matter whether they are told about heroes or gods or real people; it is the exemplars which matter. What *must* be done is to represent goodness as it is — its unchangeability, for instance. The gods must not be represented as changing or deceiving people — Zeus changing himself into a bull or anything like that. That is all very disgraceful and gives children the wrong sort of picture of what an ideal person is. And because of that, of course, he did suggest a fairly rigid censorship of the sort of stories told to young children.

When the next stage is reached the appeal is through sensory experience and concrete operations, in crafts, and manipulation of materials. Through training the eye and the touch, the individual is sensitized to the beauty of the world, and to its symmetry through his senses. Then, when emotions begin to develop in adolescence, the way in which order gets instilled is through music — good, strong Dorian music with a strong beat and a sense of order — no effeminate trills on flutes or anything like that — something with a really good rhythm to get the order, as it were, beaten into the soul. There is then gymnastics and military service to complete the training oi the body and to develop courage — again the emphasis on order. And, finally, reason which has now developed, is ready for specific treatment. The main thing, in the development of reason, is to get people to understand the principles underlying the world (in Plato's terms the Forms), to get them to concentrate on the One in the Many instead of being misled by subjective appearances and perceptual impressions of an individual kind. This is to be done by concentrating them on maths and astronomy which will give them a proper grasp of principles, of the One in the Many; for these studies provide the key to Reality. Ten years of such study should

125

purge students of subjectivity. It will avoid too much irresponsible criticizing in late adolescence before they have the first understanding of what they are meant to be criticizing. Then, after this period of settling them down to understand principles, they are ready for the dialectic proper for five years. Finally, after fifteen years' administration, hopefully, they will as it were retire to the Council of Elders and, if they are lucky, they will have a vision of the Form of the Good.

This whole process Plato described as 'turning the eye of the soul outwards towards the light'. By these various methods, starting first of all with the senses, then with the emotions and finally with more intellectual abilities, he hoped to get the individual sensitive to the Forms and to the harmony which unites the Forms, namely the Good. This, as I said, was an attempt to combine what he considered to be best in Athenian and Spartan education — the inquisitiveness, the theoretical grasp, the sensitivity of the Athenian, with the courage, discipline and order of the Spartan. A combination of what is best in these two, Plato thought, would constitute the ideal man.

2 Plato's positive contribution

So much then by way of exposition. Now what about where Plato was right? First of all I would agree with Plato that values are objective — they are not just private preferences — and that education almost by definition must be concerned with the development of valuable states of mind. There is some kind of a contradiction in what I call the specific sense of 'education'[1] in saying that a person is educated and that this is very regrettable — something bad has happened to him. Second, he thinks that education is concerned with a particular segment of what we take to be valuable in that it involves the development of understanding, and hence of reason. There are two aspects of this in Plato: first of all there are what we might call the distinct disciplines or forms of understanding and the development of arts and habits within them, in other words things like mathematics, morals, aesthetic appreciation, which are, as it were, the channels through which reason flows, and, within these there are certain abilities which can be displayed like judgment, and imagination, which have generic properties which go across the different forms of understanding, but which are or can be exhibited in all of them. So that would be the first way in which one understands the development of reason, namely the development of the different forms of understanding. Plato was particularly concerned with mathematics and morals; he had a pretty strong contempt for what we would now call physical science. He thought that actually to go and look at the world was a ridiculous way to understand it. So he did not go very far in differentiating forms of understanding.

There is also a second way of understanding the development of reason which is related to what might be called a basic level of mental health, which is to be understood in terms of minimum conditions of rationality. This is what Plato was concerned with when he talked about 'the harmony of the Soul'. In other words, given that we have desires, unless we are going to be at war within ourselves, in a state of perpetual conflict and frustration, we have to schedule them in a certain way and impose some sort of order on them. Similarly, in regard to our perception of the world, we must have some kind of realism. Being hallucinated would, for example, indicate a lack of development of reason. We have as well to be able to plan, to control, to take means to ends. All these very obvious things are connected with the elementary development of reason which is constitutive of a basic level of mental health. I think this can be made explicit by developing the sort of thing that Plato says about the harmony of the Soul. It involves holding beliefs that are not manifestly mistaken about the ordinary world; being able to plan, take means to ends, to control one's desires, to impose some sort of order on one's preferences, and so on. In this I am broadly in agreement with Plato.

Third, I agree with Plato that reason and passion are inseparable and that in education what might be called the rational passions are very important. By that I mean that, if one is seriously concerned with developing people in respect of knowledge and understanding, it is not sufficient just to stuff their heads with information. They have to develop a grasp of principles or an understanding of the Forms, but also their interest has to be awakened so that they really care, so that they have this passion for getting to the bottom of things, for getting to the explanation of what Whitehead calls 'the Forms behind the Facts'. And Whitehead regarded all philosophy as a footnote to Plato!

Now, given this positive passion to get to the bottom of things, which was manifest par excellence in Socrates, who held that the unexamined life is not worth living, which presupposes a constant striving for clarity and understanding — there are certain passions of a negative sort, which are the obverse side of this — a hatred of irrelevance, a loathing of arbitrariness, a feeling of horror if one is not clear about something. Inconsistency is intolerable and inaccuracy a vice. There are, in other words, certain intellectual virtues and vices which seem to me absolutely central to education and far too little insisted on nowadays. That is one of the things, perhaps, that a more old-fashioned classics education at least used to do for us. I am not quite sure what goes on nowadays but I once went to a classics lesson in America and the insistence was that the students should enjoy it! They were doing, I think, a piece from Seneca about a dolphin. The teacher introduced the lesson by referring to an American baseball team called The Dolphins to get them interested. Then they rattled through the piece, each taking a turn and reading the Latin in a way which made absolute gibberish of it in good rollicking style. One or two of them had a go at translating the passage. The teacher never bothered to correct them if it was obviously wrong, so I said to her afterwards 'Why on earth didn't you tell them that this was wrong?' and she said 'Oh you must not do that; they must be happy; they must enjoy it; they must not feel rejected.' I do not suggest for a moment that such practices are widespread; but there are parts of the world where classics are taught in that way. The business of actually getting the thing right is not stressed. Well, I think this shows a cavalier disregard for one of the many intellectual virtues, which are central to education.

Then in Plato there is the love of order which is central in Piaget's account also, in which the driving force of intellectual development is equilibration, the balance between assimilation and accommodation. This is a biological meta-phor for consistency; Freud, too, said that the desire for order is the basis of civilization. So there are modern parallels for the passion for order which, for Plato, underlies the whole educational system.

Finally, there is another very fruitful thought in Plato, that I think very important, which was later rediscovered as one of the latest things in sociology by G. H. Mead, namely the link between individual development and social life. Plato said that thinking is the soul's dialogue with itself and that, when the individual is thinking, what he is doing is taking into his own head a situation in which objections are put, and other points of view are represented. What we understand by 'reason' is not just a kind of gadget that we switch on in our own heads; it consists in representing, as it were, on the private screen of our own minds, a public performance in which we have taken part. It is an internalization of a form of social life. This is, I think, the very important imaginative thought that runs through Plato's whole account of the link between the development of the individual and the sort of social life in which he takes part. Plato argued, for instance, that the democratic man flourishes in a certain kind of state; the soul of the individual is mirrored in this type of social organization. The kind of social control to which a person is subjected, is very influential with regard to the development of reason. Here again there is a lot of modern sociological evidence to support him. The development of reason seems to be much affected by methods of child-rearing, for instance. If there are arbitrary methods of child-rearing, without explanation, without pointing out the consequences of action, there tends to be a stunting of the development of reason.

3 Criticism of Plato

So much, then, for Plato's positive contribution. It sounds from all this as if I am in fundamental agreement with Plato. So why then, the hesitation? What is the negative point which corresponds to the bit about the girl being pregnant in my opening story? There is no need to fuss about minor or derivative points, for instance that Plato was wrong about the distribution of human abilities, that he believed that basically most men were moronic, and that only very few were capable of understanding matters of government. That claim might be refuted by appealing to a normal distribution curve of human abilities. Similarly, there is no need to press the objections to 'noble lies' and censorship. Anyway that raises very complicated matters; for Plato had a sophisticated view of truth-telling, the role of myths, and being in a state of truth or error.

My major objection to Plato is that, although I agree with him that education is centrally concerned with the development of reason, his conception of reason is in the end indefensible. He believed that its development culminates in certainty of the sort that he found in geometry. Geometry fascinated him; this seemed to him the most amazing feature of the human mind, that human beings could, as it were, just sit and work out abstract formal systems, as the Pythagoreans did, and that these provide the basic understanding of the structure of the world. And this was *certain*; there was no room for normal human bias and fallibility in geometry. Plato thought that all reason was like this, not only in mathematics but also in morals. In morals he thought it possible for a few to have this sort of understanding of the Form of the Good. This provided the philosopher-kings with a similar kind of certainty. And if Plato was right, if in the end morality depended on the vision of the wise and there was some kind of certainty about moral issues, I think both his view of education and his political system would be very difficult to reject. But I think that this view is mistaken. It is a mistake even about mathematical reasoning, I think, and much more a mistake about reason in general.

It is necessary, therefore, fundamentally to reconceive the notion of reason, whilst still thinking of reason in a way which is consistent with the objectivity of values, but which does not entail Plato's type of dogmatism and his belief that there are people who are final authorities on matters of morals and politics as well as on mathematics. How would one begin to reconstruct an account of reason to satisfy such conditions? Well, first of all, it could be argued that the values associated with reasons are procedural, not substantive.

In other words, when one is talking about the development of reason, what is important is not *just* the attaining of particular conclusions, or of achieving some final state of understanding. Of course one needs to reach conclusions; for what is the point of enquiring about anything if one does not want to find out what is true? It is often said that we must not worry about giving children information; we must teach them how to acquire it for themselves. But if they do not acquire information in the end, what is the point of teaching them how to acquire it? And there must be some *value* in the acquiring of information, or it would be pointless to teach children how to acquire it. Similarly, there is value in getting people to understand things. But it is not just the achievement of understanding that matters; it is also the way of going about things, which includes its own values. If the development of reason is valued, then value must be accorded to consistency, to impartiality, and to those virtues — e.g. accuracy, clarity — which are conceptually connected with the pursuit of truth. Included, also, in our wider notion of reasonableness, are principles like that of freedom and respect for persons as possible sources of points of view which may be right. A certain kind of humility is also required, an acknowledgment of the possibility that anyone, above all oneself, may be in error. What matters is that one should get more and more clear about this rather than straining for the state of absolute certainty which was Plato's ideal.

Given that one gives a different account of reason along these lines, I think that one may have also to make the point that the principles involved in the use of reason are plural. There are the intellectual virtues that I have mentioned such as a love of consistency and clarity, impartiality, and a hatred of irrelevance, and arbitrariness. There are also the other virtues which provide the social context for the exercise of reason like respect for persons and freedom, without which this kind of social procedure could not in fact get off the ground. These groups of principles are plural in that there is not a slide-rule or Vision of Good by means of which conflicts can be reconciled. It seems to me, for instance, that freedom may conflict sometimes with impartiality. That there is some Vision of the Good, some one principle by

131

means of which all these different principles can be unified, I think is highly questionable, though some have looked to human happiness or to justice to perform such a unifying role.

Finally, what of the supreme value of certain goods which Plato stressed? There is, for instance, his argument for the supreme value of theoretical pursuits. A case, perhaps, can be made for saying that some sort of pursuits are qualitatively superior to others — e.g. that poetry is preferable to push-pin, to take the classic case. Types of activities may have features in virtue of which they are to be preferred to other types. But within these classes e.g. scientific pursuits as distinct from musical ones, or engineering as distinct from farming, it might be difficult to rank preferences. In other words, there may well be a kind of pluralism again with respect to goods as well as with respect to the principles which are constitutive of the use of reason.

What then are the consequences of these criticisms? First of all the account of the development of reason must be revised. There must be much more stress on criticism and on humility, on the possibility of error, on the co-operative nature of reason, which must not be viewed just as the prerogative of the élite. Second, the political institutions in which reason is immanent must be fostered. Here I agree with Plato, that you cannot expect reason to develop in a social vacuum. Social life is mirrored in the individual mind and vice versa. But I would say that it is democracy, not aristocracy, which is the articulation of reason in its social form. In this revised conception of reason, democracy is the best approximation to the social form in which reason appears. For democracy at very least involves 'parlement' or discussion, in the making of public decisions. And procedural principles such as freedom, impartiality and respect for persons, which structure the social context in which reason operates, are also principles immanent in the democratic way of life.

Note

1 See R. S. Peters, 'Education and the Educated Man', in R. F. Dearden, P. H. Hirst and R. S. Peters, *Education and the Development of Reason*, London, Routledge & Kegan Paul, 1972.

© *Didaskalos* 1975

The education of teachers

part **II**

The place of philosophy
in the 'training of teachers   7

Bacon once said that the discourses of the philosophers are
like the stars; they shed little light because they are so high. I
propose to be true to my calling in one respect at least — to
start from highly general considerations and to work my way
gradually downwards to more mundane particularities. The
stages of my coming down to earth will be marked by the following questions:
1 Why introduce educational theory at all?
2 What principles should determine the selection and presentation of theory?
3 What is meant by 'philosophy of education' as a branch of
  educational theory?
4 Which portions of 'philosophy of education' should be
  taught at the level of initial training?
5 How should philosophy of education be taught?

1   Why introduce theory at all?

There was a time, I suppose, when the view was defensible
that teachers could pick up their art entirely on an apprenticeship system from experienced practitioners on the job. Education had relatively agreed aims; procedures were more or
less standardized; few fundamental questions were raised
about principles underlying school organization, class management and the curriculum; the general standards of the community, which they were meant to pass on in training the
character of children, were relatively stable; and little was
known about the psychology of children and the social conditions under which they lived which transcended common-
sense and common-room conversation. Teachers were
gradually initiated into the tradition of teaching. And what
happened, of course, was that teachers handed on the matter
which they had acquired from their teachers in the manner

135

in which they had acquired it. There is an astonishing similarity, for instance, between how the classics were taught right up to the nineteenth century and how they were taught in ancient Rome. Teaching methods perpetuated themselves in the same sort of way as child-rearing practices in the family.

I do not want to minimize the importance of this learning on the job under skilled direction. Indeed, I think we would all agree that it must be the lynch-pin of any system of training. I need hardly comment much either on its limitations as a sufficient type of training under modern conditions. The point is that nowadays just about none of the conditions obtain which provided the milieu in which the old apprenticeship system was viable. Education no longer has agreed aims; procedures are constantly under discussion and vary according to what different people conceive themselves as doing in teaching the various subjects; fundamental questions concerned with principles underlying school organization, class management and the curriculum are constantly being raised; and in the area of moral education the task is made more perplexing by the variations of standards which characterize a highly differentiated society. The question, therefore, is not whether a modern teacher indulges in philosophical reflection about what he is doing; it is rather whether he does it in a sloppy or in a rigorous manner.

Similarly, our knowledge about the psychology of children and about the historical and social conditions which affect their behaviour and the organization of schools has vastly increased. There may be two — or more than two — opinions about how much has been definitely established in these areas. But there can be no two opinions about the extent to which work in these areas has developed and percolated through to people at all levels in society. The teacher can no longer rely on experience, common-sense, and common-room conversation about such matters, if he is going to hold his own against vociferous and intelligent parents and against every type of 'expert' who is advising him what should be done with children. A working knowledge of these sciences of man is becoming as essential to a teacher as a knowledge of anatomy and physiology is to a doctor. Education is becoming increasingly a matter of public concern and public scrutiny. Unless teachers are well versed in these sciences which are ancillary to their task there is little hope of their establishing themselves as a profession which can retain some kind of authority in the community. Again the question is not whether the teacher has opinions on psychological, sociological or historical matters; for any educated person has these. It is rather whether he can defend his opinions in an informed and intelligent way so that he can hold his own in the welter of public discussion. The simple truth, in other words, is that the teacher has to learn to think for himself about what he is doing. He can no longer rely on an established tradition. A beginning must therefore be made at the level of initial training to equip him with the rudiments of disciplined philosophical thought and with those parts of psychology and the social sciences which are of particular relevance to his complex task. For though those who come to us are presumed to be educated in a general sense, very few of them have more than a nodding acquaintance with those particular disciplines that are ancillary to their task.

There is a further point too. It could well be argued that though the main emphasis at the level of initial training must be on the *training* of teachers, we cannot altogether neglect our duty as educators to educate them as persons. Philosophy, psychology, history and the social sciences play a vital role in what may be called a liberal education under modern conditions. I remember vividly the occasion on which I first went to see Dean Keppel on my arrival as Visiting Professor at the Harvard Graduate School of Education. He told me explicitly that, though he wanted me to relate philosophy to education, he was also most concerned that I should teach the students in the MAT programme some *philosophy* as part of their general education as human beings. To quote the stated rationale of this one year programme which, it is claimed, has already done much to improve the quality of teachers in High Schools in the States:

> The preparation of teachers depends upon three major elements: a basic general education in the liberal tradition, a thorough grasp of one or more academic disciplines

137

taught in the schools, and an intellectual and practical introduction to a career in education which includes an internship or apprenticeship.

This double aspect of the role of disciplines bearing on education naturally introduces my second question: 'What principles should be adopted for the selection and presentation of theory at this level?' to which I will now proceed.

2 Principles for selection and presentation of theory

This dual aspect of the role of theory is constantly present to a person trained in one of the basic disciplines such as philosophy, or history, who has to contribute to a course which is primarily vocational in its emphasis. On the one hand he is under pressure from others, and perhaps also from his own inclinations or sense of obligation, to add the voice of his discipline to the conversation on topics which are of practical importance to teachers. On the other hand he wishes to initiate others into a form of thinking whose direction is dictated by the autonomous standards of discipline itself and not at all by the interests and needs of a particular profession. He has a loyalty to the tradition of his own discipline, with its built-in standards of rigour, as well as to the Institution which employs him, and it is a nice point as to how much he will be prepared to simplify and to curb his passion for problems within his own discipline in favour of concerns which are practically urgent but theoretically uninteresting. To give a parallel: philosophers are often asked to lecture on the ethics of marriage. Now marriage presents plenty of practical and moral problems, as most of us know. But the fundamental ethical problems to which it may give rise depend in no way on particular institutional provisions or on those concrete clashes of principles which occasion moral conflicts. They are much better discussed by dealing more abstractly with the merits of an intuitionist, Kantian, or Utilitarian ethical theory. In a similar way there is a wide-spread practical problem in education about one's attitude to pop music rather than classical or to games rather than science, art, or literature. The fundamental philosophical issues raised by such questions were discussed by Mill in his *Utilitarianism* and by Moore in his *Principia Ethica*. They can only be solved at this highly abstract level. But in a vocational setting, such as that of initial training, what is a teacher to do?

The answer, I think, derives from a possible extension of the notion of a 'liberal education'. This usually suggests the refusal to harness disciplines to any practical or utilitarian ends; the determination to explore them for their own sake and to pursue paths intimated by what is internal to the disciplines themselves. But, I would suggest, it could also be extended so that one could describe a vocational training as liberally or illiberally conceived and implemented. This would pick out the extent to which the disciplines relevant to practical ends — e.g. sciences such as psychology and sociology in the case of education — are taught only under this practical aspect rather than in such a way as constantly to lead students to get a glimmering of the fundamental problems in the disciplines which are at issue even if they have neither the time nor the equipment to explore them in a rigorous manner. In the case of education and politics there is a further reason why disciplines must be presented in this liberal way; for neither education nor politics are useful arts or branches of technology in any straightforward sense in the way in which some might claim that medicine and engineering are. For though they are practical in character their theory cannot be adequately conceived of as related to any agreed or non-controversial ends. This, by the way, is one of the reasons which makes them both philosophically interesting in ways in which engineering is not.

There is, however, a third principle which is presupposed by my other two principles, that is that 'education' is not a distinct discipline but a field where a group of disciplines have application. In this respect it is rather like politics. 'Education', as a legitimate and fruitful field of study, has suffered too much from people who cannot distinguish the sort of questions they are asking and who are not equipped in the disciplines relevant to answering them. Talks that go down well at speech-days and conferences are too often mistaken for the sort of thing which could count as a contribution to educational theory. Logically speaking all questions

139

of educational policy and practice are hybrid questions, a crossing of value judgments with different forms of empirical enquiry. So the first step towards answering such questions must be the breaking down of the questions into their logically distinct components. If, for instance, we want to know whether we ought to punish children, the ethical issues of principle must be distinguished from the psychological and social questions about causes and consequences. But once the various voices that speak about education, emanating from the different disciplines, have been separated out and trained, they need to join together in an orderly and coherent conversation about matters of common concern to teachers and practical administrators. In brief, we must make an end of the undifferentiated mush that is often perpetrated under the heading of educational theory before the different types of question have been distinguished; but we must make sure that the research and training carried out under the aegis of the different disciplines is brought together again in an integrated conversation on matters of common concern. In fact I am making in a concrete way the logical point that 'integration' is inseparable from 'differentiation'.

There would thus seem to be three main principles determining the selection and presentation of educational theory:

(1) Though it must be presented in a differentiated way the different disciplines must also mesh in with and be seen to mesh in with each other in relation to matters of educational policy and practice.

(2) Selection from the content of the basic disciplines must, in the main, be determined by what is relevant to the practical problems and interests of teachers in training.

(3) The differentiated modes of thought about education, though harnessed to practical issues, must also be presented in a way that they intimate, and are seen to intimate, problems at a more fundamental level in the disciplines themselves, and the forms of enquiry necessary for their solution.

An 'education' course, therefore, which implemented these basic principles, would seem to be one in which a common core of problems or topics were selected which were dealt with concurrently from the point of view of the different disciplines. For instance 'equality' or 'authority and social control' would be tackled concurrently by the philosopher, the psychologist, and the sociologist. The analysis and discussion would be related closely to the practical problems of teachers in schools. The topics would be tackled in such a way that the students were led to see gradually how, in each case, fundamental problems in the basic disciplines themselves are involved.

I will now pass to problems specific to the teaching of philosophy of education. Most of what I say will be merely a matter of applying the general principles which I have just attempted to formulate.

3   What is meant by 'philosophy of education' as a branch of educational theory?

'Philosophy of education', like 'philosophy', suggests rather different things to different people. To the general public, perhaps, it suggests high-level directives for living in general or education in particular, derived from deep probings into or ponderings on the meaning of life. To the professional philosopher, on the other hand, it intimates the disciplined demarcation of concepts and the patient explication of the grounds of knowledge and conduct. Philosophers nowadays ally themselves with Socrates and Kant in asking and trying to answer the questions 'What do you mean?', 'How do you know?' and 'What must we presuppose?'. There has been a revolution in philosophy during this century and one of its main features has been an increased awareness of what philosophy is and is not.

For a time philosophers were so concerned with their revolution and so preoccupied with central questions in logic, theory of knowledge, metaphysics, and ethics, that they were comparatively oblivious of what was going on in other fields. The climate of opinion is now very different. Many philosophers, who have been brought up in the 'revolution', are now turning, with sharper and more highly polished tools, to problems in law, politics, art, psychology, psycho-analysis, social science — and education. They are thus rather aghast when they encounter what is often called 'philosophy of

141

education' with its rather woolly chatter about 'growth', 'wholeness', 'maturity', 'discipline', 'experience', 'creativeness', 'needs', 'interests' and 'freedom'. They are even more aghast when they learn that students very often are brought up on an antiquated diet of Plato, Rousseau, and Froebel — perhaps with a dash of Dewey to provide a final obfuscation of issues. It is as if a course on educational psychology consisted mainly in snippets from Aristotle, Locke, James Mill, Herbart, and Thorndike.

Of course lecturers in Colleges of Education and University Departments of Education are not greatly to blame for this, for the fact is that philosophers to date have done almost nothing in this country to help matters. But this will soon, we hope, be remedied. This year, for instance, the Manchester UP are bringing out a collection of lectures given on *Aims in Education* — contributed mainly by English philosophers. Routledge & Kegan Paul are also bringing out a collection of articles entitled *Philosophical Analysis and Education* (1965). I myself am desperately trying to write an introductory book entitled *Ethics and Education* and Mr. Hirst, one of my colleagues at the London Institute, is also trying to write a book on *The Philosophical Foundations of the Curriculum*. The problem is to find the time, with the pressure of administration and teaching increasing every term, to put on paper what we have in our heads.

What, then, is there to be done in the philosophy of education? It can be roughly characterized as the application of (i) philosophy of mind (ii) ethics and social philosophy (iii) theory of knowledge, to educational issues. Let me explain this in a bit more detail:

(1) *Philosophy of mind*, which is often called philosophical psychology. A great deal of work has to be done here on the demarcation of concepts falling under 'education' such as 'training', 'indoctrination', 'teaching', 'conditioning', together with the concept of 'education' itself. Then there are concepts such as 'experience', 'interests', 'needs', 'maturity', 'growth', 'mental health', which are so often bandied about in discussions of educational aims and procedures. There are also more general problems to do with the conceptual schemes employed by educational psychologists in theorizing about human nature.

(2) *Ethics and social philosophy*. In this area there arise the crucial problems of justification as well as problems of analysis. There are assumptions about the aims of education and about worthwhile content which require justification. There are also assumptions about the desirability of the procedures by means of which this is to be transmitted. Problems of content raise the age-old issue of the desirability of poetry rather than push-pin; problems of procedure raise issues to do with liberty, equality, authority, and punishment. What is meant by these terms? How are the underlying principles to be justified? How do they have application in the school situation?

(3) *Theory of knowledge*. There are all sorts of philosophical problems connected with the curriculum. In so far as education involves the transmission of differentiated forms of thought such as science, history, morals, and mathematics, the philosophy of these forms of thought is obviously relevant. What is distinctive about their conceptual schemes? What forms of reasoning do they employ? Then there is the problem of the logical aspects of forms of thought in relation to the psychology of learning. There are questions about the relationship of school 'subjects' to forms of thought, about the 'integration' of the curriculum, and 'liberal education'. There are questions, too, about the contribution of the curriculum to moral education and the education of the emotions.

4 Which portions of the philosophy of education should be taught at the level of initial training?

It is one thing to enunciate a programme of work to be done in the philosophy of education; it is quite another to determine in detail which parts of it are suitable for study at the level of initial training. For we must be mindful of the principles determining the selection and presentation of theory in general which are:
(1) possibility of 'meshing-in' with other disciplines
(2) relevance to practical problems and interests of teachers in training

(3) desirability of leading on to fundamental problems in philosophy itself.

(2) Let us start with the second principle of selection. There are bound to be differences here according to the age-range of the children whom the teacher is being trained to teach. Discipline and problems to do with the nature of school-subjects, for instance, tend to be much more live issues for secondary than for primary teachers, whereas an emphasis on the needs and interests of children and the collection of philosophical issues to do with 'child-centred' education is much more marked at the primary level. I have found, with all classes of teachers in initial training, that the following topics usually get a lively response:

(a) What is 'education'? What should be its aims? What is the teacher meant to be doing qua teacher? How is education different from training? How can civilized activities such as science and poetry be justified?

(b) Problems to do with the authority of the teacher.

(c) The ethics of punishment and discipline.

(d) The concept of 'child-centred' education, together with notions such as learning from experience, and gearing the curriculum to the needs and interests of children.

(e) Freedom — of the child and of the teacher.

(f) Equality in education.

(g) Moral education.

(1) In relation to the first principle — all the topics mentioned above are excellent ones for 'meshing-in' with psychology and sociology. In dealing with equality, for instance, the analysis and justification of 'equality' as a principle can be excellently illuminated by sociological facts about social class and social mobility and by psychological investigations of the determinants of intelligence and aptitude, streaming, and linguistic ability.

I should like to insert a special plea here for the importance of philosophy in this 'meshing' operation. Students are often brought up on too one-sided a diet purveyed by those with predominantly psychological interests. The result is that they can come to feel guilty about using common-sense. Our Director H. L. Elvin once initiated a discussion with some third-year students at a Training College by asking them the following questions: 'If you were taking a class which was beginning to get out of hand because of the disruptive influence of a rebellious boy, which thoughts would come into your minds: "How can I restore the rule of law in this class?" or "I wonder what that boy's home background is." ' They answered: 'The first sorts of thoughts, but we would feel *guilty* about it: for all we learn at College is to do with the second sorts of thoughts!' One need not delve very deeply into the complexities of 'authority' and 'punishment' to realize that these teachers had been brought up on a one-sided diet! They lacked an adequate rationale for what they were doing. Similarly one often comes across disillusioned primary teachers who have been nurtured rather delicately by psychologically-orientated lectures in the ideology of activity methods, who have found themselves in tough situations where they simply could not apply them. They were at a loss what to do and developed a hard-bitten contempt for those who trained them. What they lacked was the rationale underlying such methods which would permit intelligent adaptation to diverse circumstances. They lacked what Aristotle called an understanding of 'the reason why' of things. Perhaps, too, they were brought up on a widely prevalent but quite unrealistic model of an educational situation which envisages one teacher dealing with one child!

(3) From the point of view of the third criterion some topics are far better than others. The ethics of punishment, for instance, or 'equality' provide excellent avenues into the fundamental issues of moral philosophy; the analysis of 'education' itself is an excellent introduction to conceptual analysis and leads readily into ethical issues to do with the justification of what is worth while handing on. But it may well be that other topics satisfy the other two principles better. At this level of teaching the philosophy of education there is a constant tension between attempting to illuminate and clarify concrete issues so that teachers can go about their business in a more clear-headed way, and drawing them deeper into the discipline so that they can begin to develop a distinctive form of thought which will entail a more rigorous overhaul of their fundamental beliefs and ideals. The effectiveness of teaching philosophy at this level will be

revealed both in the autonomy, and critical experimental attitude which teachers begin to show in the latter stages of
teaching practice, as well as in their desire to return to the
philosophy of education in a more rigorous way when they
are established as teachers.

So much for the attempt to work out a conception of the
content of philosophy of education at the level of initial
training which is consistent with the underlying principles for
the teaching of theory in general which I have tried to formulate. It would seem, however, if the London Institute of
Education is to be regarded as being in any way representative
of what goes on in the country as a whole, my views about
the content of philosophy of education are somewhat at
variance with current practice. Before committing my
thoughts on this topic to paper I conducted a very modest
little survey to find out what actually goes on under this
heading in our thirty odd colleges. I found that the subject
is approached in practically every case from the point of view
of the history of educational ideas. This is often supplemented
by tackling philosophical problems as they arise in general
undifferentiated education seminars which are related to
students' problems and interests. This way of tackling the
subject reflects, of course, the qualifications of staff. I also
found in my survey that it is only a small minority of colleges who have a real philosophy specialist on the staff
whereas more than half of them have staff with specialist
qualifications which include the history of ideas.

The question, however, is whether this historical type of
approach is the *best* approach. Is it easy both to do justice to
Plato, Locke, Rousseau, and Froebel and to make what they
said really relevant to the problems of the modern teacher? Is
it easy to 'mesh-in' this sort of approach with that of the
psychologist and sociologist to a common core of problems?
In other words can this type of approach really satisfy my
first two principles of selection and presentation? There is no
doubt that it can satisfy the third. If one were simply concerned with teaching students philosophy there is a great deal
to be said for the historical approach, though many philosophers would disagree even with this. There is, of course, a lot
to be said for such courses as background courses and as part

146

of the history of education course. We do, after all, want teachers to be educated as well as trained. But the question is whether the main *emphasis* should be on this approach at the level of initial training. In our postgraduate certificate course at the Central London Institute we have had to sacrifice this historical sweep in the interests of integration and practical relevance. It now features as a compulsory paper for every-one taking the Academic Diploma. They have to do a General Theory paper which consists in a study of the relevance to education of the ideas of the following: Plato, Rousseau, Dewey, Freud, Piaget, Skinner, Durkheim, and Mannheim. At the level of initial training cannot a lot of this historical material too easily become what Whitehead called 'inert ideas'?

An advantage of the historical approach is, of course, that there are books readily available on which the course can be based. But this is a temporary and contingent matter which should not be allowed to dictate the way in which a subject is taught. Please don't misunderstand me! I am not arguing that students should be discouraged from reading *The Repub-lic* or *Emile* — even *Democracy and Education*, if they can make anything of it! I am suggesting that the course should be orientated to a core of practical problems which can be clarified by philosophical thinking. These books should be consulted, like any others, in so far as they are relevant. But they should not dictate the form of the course. We often argue that the school curriculum should be carefully related to the needs and interests of children and to their level of cognitive development. Should not the same apply to courses for students in training?

5   How should the philosophy of education be taught?

There is little that can be said in a general sort of way about the detailed implementation of such a conception of the philosophy of education. For it must depend so much on contingent circumstances that vary from college to college and department to department. Most of the work done must be in small seminars taken by tutors who have no specialist training in philosophy. This is one of the facts of life from which any realistic scheme must start. But there should be at

147

least one specialist in philosophy of education on every staff. And by that I mean someone with a training in philosophy, not in the history of ideas. He or she can devise a course in consultation with colleagues who have to take the seminars and with other specialists with whose courses his has to be integrated. The exercise, in other words, must approximate to an example of team teaching.

I am a firm believer in such foundation courses, provided that they are followed up by teaching seminars based on them, whose tutors have, if possible, also attended the courses. It is often argued that the skilled tutor can deal out of his own head with topics in philosophy, psychology, and social aspects of education as they arise in undifferentiated seminars, without the aid of such courses. This may be so with very gifted tutors if they have plenty of time and small groups of students. But, in general, I don't believe it. For students cannot begin to think in a rigorous differentiated way without being given the conceptual tools and without the forms of argument being articulated for them by one well versed in this form of thought, so that they can gradually pick it up. People do not learn precision of thought by the light of nature; they have to be taught it by one who is skilled at it. A good course of lectures provides an indispensable structure for the discussions of topics; it signposts the questions to be answered. It maps the lines of argument which are relevant to answering them. As most education tutors are only likely to be well versed in one form of thought themselves, which is relevant to education, some form of team-teaching is surely the only realistic way to proceed. For lectures, which are not followed up by small seminars or tutorials, are only of limited value.

I am postulating by the way, in case you are somewhat uneasy at my talk of 'specialists', be they philosophers or psychologists, that they must also have had practical experience of teaching. They must know, from first-hand experience, what the battle-field is like. I shudder at the thought of importing pure philosophers or psychologists from University departments, to put on such courses, if they have never tried to take a class of children themselves. The difficulty, as is well known, is to get staff who are both experienced teachers and also trained in one or more of the foundation disciplines of philosophy, psychology, and sociology. We are only making a beginning with training such specialists at London with our new MA by examination which is likely soon to be a one year rather than a two year fulltime course after the Academic Diploma.

A final word about seminars. I am a firm believer in them provided they are small in size and involve both participation and preparation. There is, of course, some value in people coming together and learning to share their experience in groups. I am not one to argue against the virtues of group-therapy. Indeed some seminars I have been present at in the Subject Departments during teaching practice approximate very closely to fruitful sessions of 'Alcoholics Anonymous'. But education is rather different from therapy in that it involves gradual initiation into rigorous and differentiated modes of thought and awareness. This necessitates preparation as well as participation. Written work is one of the best methods of preparation if it provides a focus for thought and reading. For one does not often know what one thinks about an issue until one has had to state one's thoughts clearly and defend them. One makes a view *one's own* in this way as well as by committing oneself in action.

In case you may think that my suggestions are somewhat dreamy or wildly impracticable I will end by giving a brief sketch of the system which we have recently worked out at London in the Central College for education courses at the post-graduate certificate level of Initial Training.

Counting Music and Arts students we train about 450 students a year. Each student belongs, basically, to a tutorial group in a Subject Department — e.g. History, Art, English and all his or her subject work and teaching practice is conducted in connexion with this tutorial group. Each group has one tutor, the size being about 12 students. In this they tackle the philosophy of their own subjects as well as problems to do with methods of teaching it. Each student also belongs to an Education Group which, we hope, will consist of about 15 students recruited across the Subject Departments. Each such Education Group has three specialist or semi-specialist tutors attached to it in philosophy, psychology,

and social aspects of education, many of whom are also subject tutors. The work of these groups consists in seminars,
individual tutorials, and written work which is all geared to
lecture courses in the three foundation disciplines. These lectures tackle an agreed common core of educational problems
concurrently from the standpoint of the distinct disciplines.
The tutors meet with the lecturers at the beginning and end
of the course to discuss how things are going and to plan
general matters of policy. At the end of the course there will
be lectures on current educational issues — e.g. streaming, the
future of independent schools, the school curriculum —
which will be followed up by meetings of the Education
Groups at which, it is hoped, all three specialists will be
present. The idea of this is to end the course by bringing together, in relation to controversial issues, the differentiated
forms of thinking that have been running together in harness
during the previous part of the course. During the Spring
and Summer each student has also to take an optional subject, which can be philosophy of education, educational psychology, history of education, sociology of education, or
comparative education. The teaching for this — lectures and
seminars — is conducted by specialists in the Education
Departments.

I am well aware that at the London Central Institute conditions prevail that are unusual, perhaps unparalleled, in the
country as a whole. But I do not see why the principles
underlying the course cannot be applied more widely. They
probably are. If anyone were to ask about the success of this
system of tackling the Education Course I would reply that
our scheme is still in a fairly experimental stage. I would
want to know also how 'success', both short-term and long-
term, is to be assessed. But that itself would be a very suitable subject both for differentiated and integrated thought
about education!

© R. S. Peters 1964

'Education' as a specific preparation for teaching   8

1 The priority of content

If anything is to be regarded as a specific preparation for teaching, priority must be given to a thorough grounding in something to teach. There are other things which a teacher must know as well — about children, for instance, and the social conditions which shape their lives. But social workers, therapists, and juvenile employment officers must also know about these things. A teacher, in so far as he is concerned with teaching and not just with therapy, 'socialization', or advice about careers, must have mastered something which he can impart to others. Without this he would be like an actor who was exquisitely sensitive to the reactions of an audience, a master of gesture and of subtle inflexions of voice, but who omitted to do one thing — to learn his words.

In order to safeguard myself from being thought a reactionary formalist with an itch to pin children down on forms, let me straight away remove an obvious possibility of misunderstanding. 'Teaching', as I understand it, includes a host of activities that have in common the structuring of a situation in such a way that something can be learnt. This can involve formal methods of instruction or informal ways of arranging things so that children will be led to find out things for themselves. I have only one major conviction about methods of teaching — that no over-all generalizations about it are possible. Everything depends upon what is being taught, to whom, by whom, and to how many. I recently went over a primary school where the free day had been instituted. After being told all about the educational value of each child choosing its own activity I was promptly taken to see a splendid class-singing lesson in progress — an admirable piece of formal instruction by a professional singer who was also a trained teacher. To my surprise the headmistress purred over it. But who could not when witnessing such a superb piece of teaching? And, after all, there are differences between music and reading — and people's educational practices are often very much at variance with their avowed principles.

I myself started my educational career with a three year stint in one of the most informal of all educational institutions — a youth centre. When I became a secondary school-teacher I found it dead easy compared with what I had been doing. Ever since I have retained the conviction that informal methods, at any level, are much more demanding of the teacher than more formal methods. What is demanded is not simply efficiency of organization and a grasp of what is going on outside the teaching space, but also knowledge and understanding that is available at any time — not just after one has managed to look it all up. I heard of some students recently who were sent to observe an experienced teacher using informal methods of stimulating children's questions — an admirable way of teaching, if one can manage it, in any situation, whether formal or informal. They were dogged searchers after truth, these students; so they kept a minute-by-minute record of what actually transpired in her teaching space. They found that out of thirty questions demanding an informative answer in a given period she was only able to deal adequately with five of them! It is true that she often told the unsatisfied children where to go and look to find answers. But most of the children did not bother and the teacher was usually unable to check on whether they did or not. The reason for this unintentional thwarting of the children's desire to learn was partly the need for controlling the other children and dealing with their constant demands of a non-educational nature (in my view this method of teaching would be enormously aided by the employment of auxiliaries to deal with such demands which must obtrude themselves in a class of over twenty); but it was also partly due to the unpredictable demands on the teacher's knowledge in such an unstructured situation. We all know how much easier it is to give a good lecture than to take a really good seminar in which most of those present participate in some kind of guided exploration. In the latter case the guide has to know the territory much better. One of my most sobering experiences in teaching was the first time I lectured on Hegel — a philosopher whom I confess I have never properly understood. On that occasion I understood almost nothing about what he was getting at — yet afterwards I was congratulated by one or two students on giving a brilliant lecture!

And so we return to the point from which I started — the necessity, whatever methods are used, of a thorough grounding in something to teach. Too frequently one hears heads nowadays say things like 'I am not fussy about the methods young teachers use. After all there are all sorts of experiments going on and they have to try them out. But the trouble is that they do not really understand the stuff they are meant to be teaching.' This mastery of content is more than ever necessary nowadays in the light of various attempts to develop a topic-centred curriculum in some junior and comprehensive schools. For my impression is that if such experiments are to prove more than a new set of gimmicks, they will require a *more* thorough grasp of the forms of thinking that are to be so integrated than the more traditional subject-centred curriculum.

2 Contribution of 'education' to curriculum courses

To get to the main source of the teacher's mastery — or lack of mastery of content — would involve discovering precisely what goes on in Colleges under the heading of 'Curriculum Courses'. This, as anyone knows who has tried to penetrate these mysteries, is no mean undertaking, and certainly outside my main terms of reference. But a few thoughts about these arcana are necessary for the development of my thesis about the 'education' component of the course.

It is also necessary in the light of what I have already said about the importance of content; for as there prevails in most Colleges the doctrine, whose rationale I have always found bewildering, that an 'academic' subject which she may never have to teach can be studied for the 'personal development' of a primary teacher, the onus of providing a grounding for what has to be taught falls on those responsible for curriculum courses. And here we come face to face with the situation

which to my mind is often as acute a source of embarrass-
ment, insecurity, and conflict in Colleges of Education as sex
once was and class now is in society at large. It is this: those
who have a thorough understanding of mathematics, science,
social studies, music, English, religion, and so on, tend to be
those whose teaching experience has predominantly been
with older children. Yet, if they are responsible for curriculum courses, they have to instruct students in how to teach
these subjects to younger children about whose minds they
know very little. Education lecturers, on the other hand,
know plenty about small children but their knowledge of
subjects is usually pretty rudimentary. Indeed they are
sometimes not above rationalizing their ignorance by pro-
claiming that there are no distinct ways of being aware of the
world. They are right, of course, about the minds of young
children and about primitive peoples whose beliefs are comparatively undifferentiated. But they are not right about the
minds of educated people since the Enlightenment. Indeed
one of the great achievements of eighteenth-century philosophers, such as Hume and Kant, was to show conclusively that
empirical science is different in important respects from
mathematics, and that morals is not mainly a matter either
of demonstrative or of empirical reasoning.

There are, however, important educational truths contained in this stress on wholeness. In the first place we would
not call a person educated whose understanding was narrowly
specialized in one way of viewing the world — who saw a car
only as a piece of machinery without aesthetic grace, without
a history, and without potentialities for human good and ill.
In the second place forms of understanding make use of each
other — physics of mathematics, history of the social sciences,
and moral judgments of psychological understanding. These
ways of stressing 'wholeness' are quite consistent with the
differentiation of mind into those forms of understanding
into which it is the business of modern teachers gradually to
initiate another generation.

This stress on 'integration' provides a clue also both to
how this problem of the dichotomy between knowledge of
subjects and knowledge of children can be dealt with, especially in a large College, and to one of the main functions of

the 'education' course. It is my conviction that curriculum courses, together with teaching practice, provide a fine opportunity for fruitful collaboration between education and subject specialists which would do much to provide a more thorough grounding for students in the content and methods of the various curriculum subjects. It should also ease some of the tensions and insecurities that now exist in many Colleges. Each age range could have a team drawn partly from subject specialists and partly from education specialists. In the teaching of science, for instance, at the Junior level there would be a subject specialist trained in science together with an education lecturer familiar with Piaget's and Bruner's work on the development of scientific concepts; it is hoped, too, that one or other of them would have thought about the philosophy of science and about the point of teaching it. And so on with the other subjects. Indeed I would like to cement the bonds even more closely by encouraging subject lecturers to do in-service training on child development and the philosophy of education and education lecturers to do in-service courses on the relevant curriculum subjects. Each lecturer would have, of course, his basic loyalty to his education or subject department. But he would have also a subsidiary loyalty to an age range team responsible for curriculum courses and teaching practice, thereby institutionalizing an integration which ought gradually to develop in the minds of all concerned.

It might be objected that I am laying too much stress on subject content and too little on the development of each individual child. But this would be to misunderstand my position. For I would maintain that it is impossible to characterize what is *meant* by 'development' without reference to the ways of being aware of the world and of other people — moral, interpersonal, scientific, aesthetic, historical, religious — which are constitutive of the development of mind. What we call 'school-subjects' may be highly contingent affairs, depending on convenience and historical traditions. But forms of awareness, each with their own types of truth-criteria and methods of validation, are not so contingent. They represent the main ways in which man has learnt to make sense of the world and to organize his reactions to it. Within these forms

155

of awareness there is plenty of scope for individual emphasis and originality. But these individual interpretations have always to be understood as offshoots which are nourished by our common heritage. What I am arguing for, in other words, is a new approach to child-development that takes a more systematic account of the early stages of these basic forms of awareness instead of perpetuating absurd categorizations such as 'intellectual', 'social', 'moral', and 'emotional'. I am also arguing with equal vehemence against the practice of teaching 'subjects' to students without making any serious attempt to relate them to a proper understanding of how the minds of small children work.

Were my terms of reference wider I would like to examine dispassionately the wisdom of insisting that all primary teachers study one main subject in depth, for their 'personal development', as under the present system. (Is there an implication in this that learning how to teach is *not* part of their 'personal development'?) In many ways an alternative scheme of making it possible for some to have a thorough liberal education in the main areas of the primary curriculum — science, mathematics, English, social studies, and one of the arts — together with a thorough knowledge of how to teach these subjects at the appropriate level — would have much to commend it. But such a suggestion might seem rather visionary in the light of the pressures likely to be exerted on teacher training by the coming of the BEd. My fear is that the various factors of prestige which this will involve will lead to an even more drastic down-grading of curriculum courses than prevails at the moment. Yet if the new Middle School gets off the ground, there is likely to be a growing demand for teachers to have a much more thorough knowledge than they have at the moment of at least these main areas of the curriculum. The alternative, which would be in line with BEd development, would be to bring the specialization of the Secondary School well down into the Middle School. It seems probable that both sorts of development will occur under different authorities depending on the extent to which the Infant approach is pushed up into the Middle School or the Secondary type of approach is pushed down. But, whichever type of alternative is adopted, the need for something more thorough than existing curriculum courses for Junior/Secondary students is surely inescapable.

This, then, in my view would be the first priority for 'education' as a specific preparation for teaching — collaboration with subject specialists in curriculum courses and teaching practice in order to provide a firm and solid foundation for the basic task of any teacher — that of helping a new generation to make something of themselves by the development of those forms of understanding and awareness which are constitutive of what it means to be 'educated'.

3   The teaching of skills

My next priority for 'education' as a specific preparation for teaching would be a thorough grounding in teaching the skills — reading, spelling, and writing, especially reading, which is one of the 'basic needs' of any child in our culture. Joyce Morris's work has made us familiar enough with the deficiencies in this sphere of the preparation of many Junior teachers. But the Infant teachers who have sent up so many illiterates from their classes cannot be altogether absolved from responsibility for their plight. My wife, who runs a remedial clinic for backward children, is impressed by the number of children referred to her whose difficulties derive from poor instruction at an early stage. This state of affairs has come to be not only because of well-meaning woolliness about 'reading-readiness' but also because of sheer lack of training in the teaching of skills. Typical of such a combination was a case she came across the other day where a young teacher had been appointed to an Infant school in a reasonably good area. The headmaster found that he had to spend a lot of his time in her first term explaining to her how to use the basic reading methods with children who were eager to read. She knew plenty about preparing the environment so as to get children ready for reading but absolutely nothing about passing on the reading process itself. On enquiry, it transpired that the poor girl had had only one lecture on reading at her College. This consisted mainly in an elaboration of the theme that children would pick up reading naturally when they were 'ready' for it. Educational theory is littered with such half-truths which are paraded as panaceas.

4 General theory of education

And so we come to what is often called 'general theory of
education' as distinct from that part of it which is concerned with the logical and psychological aspects of teaching
the different subjects — and with the content of the skills
that are necessary conditions for development within them.
In this area, since the Hull conference in 1964, there has been
a steady move away from what I once called the 'undifferentiated mush' of the educational theory of the past and an
attempt to approach general problems of teaching and learning in a more precise and informed way from the standpoint
of the distinct disciplines of philosophy, psychology, sociology, and history which, logically speaking, contribute to
them. I need not go over all that again — especially as you
can now find this conception of educational theory elabora-
ted in the book called *The Study of Education* edited by
Professor Tibble and published by Routledge & Kegan Paul. I
am often worried, however, about what may happen to education courses if they get into the hands of those who are too
zealous about their own specialisms and too intolerant of
past traditions — especially if they have the stick of the BEd
which they can brandish over the head of their bemused students. Already one hears cases of philosophers and sociologists, with little understanding of primary schools or of the
minds of the students they teach, slapping on formal courses
in their own disciplines too early, in too abstract a manner,
and without the students being rendered ready for them. You
need no reminding, I am sure, that many psychologists have
carried on in this sort of way ever since the much earlier time
when psychology came to be conceived of as a distinct part
of the education course!

There is also the very important matter of 'integration',
which I have already referred to in the context of relating the
teaching of 'education' closely to curriculum subjects. This
applies also to the desirability of keeping together the philosophical, psychological and sociological components of educational theory. Even if topics are treated in an increasingly
differentiated way as the course proceeds, there is no reason
why a central core of topics should not be selected to which

all branches of educational theory can contribute and which can be dealt with from these different points of view. In this way students would gradually be provided with the tools for working out what they themselves think about the problems that confront them and they would not be brought up on a one-sided diet like the staple diet which was all that was available when psychology was the only part of educational theory which had been differentiated out. I can do no better at this point than quote from what I have written elsewhere to summarize my views about these aspects of the 'education' course. This was written from the point of view of the contribution of philosophy to educational theory but it applies to other branches as well:

With prospective teachers undergoing a course of initial training the situation is very different. For philosophy has to be taught in such a way that it gradually transforms their outlook and manner of approach to educational problems. It would be most unfortunate if, in a genuine attempt to get rid of clichés and woolliness of thought, formalized courses were introduced which dealt with matters beyond the interest and experience of students who simply swotted up a 'subject' in order to pass an examination.

In order to avoid the danger of philosophy becoming a corpus of inert ideas it must arise naturally from the student's developing experience in training. Philosophical questions must gradually be differentiated out from the practical and personal problems encountered in schools. These problems — e.g., those of discipline, teaching methods, and the organization of the school — have psychological and social aspects as well. It would be desirable, therefore, if the different forms of thinking which contribute to educational theory could be differentiated out gradually in relation to a common corpus of practical problems. Gradually, as the student develops in maturity and begins to get accustomed to the different ways of thinking about these problems, he or she will be able to go deeper into the contributing disciplines and will be ready for more formal courses in them. For there comes a time when what Whitehead calls 'the stage of precision' is reached. It is one thing to develop an interest in problems and to begin to grasp what the problems are; but it is quite another thing to develop the mental apparatus necessary for tackling them with clarity and precision. This takes a very long time and only a beginning can be made with it in Initial Training. It is hoped that with the coming of the BEd students will be able, in their fourth year, to develop some precision of thought in at least one of the disciplines which contribute to educational theory.

The educational course as a whole can surely be viewed as a kind of spiral in which, as the years proceed, a range of problems keep on cropping up and can be treated with more and more depth and differentiation. Questions such as 'Should children be punished at school?' or 'What is the educational significance of play?' or 'Can morality be taught?' or 'When should children learn to read?' can be answered at all sorts of different levels. They could form the subject of discussions with students early on in an education course in which students are scarcely aware of the distinction between philosophical and psychological questions. Or they could be treated as dissertation topics at MA level. As students proceed up the spiral of the education course they should keep on coming round to problems that they have encountered before. But as they develop they should begin to be more and more sensitive to the different types of question that are concealed in these general problems, and their understanding of them should be both broadened and deepened by a proper combination of theory with practice.

In the three year course we are primarily concerned with turning out good teachers, not with training philosophers, psychologists, or sociologists. The most we can hope for is that teachers will be increasingly sensitized to these different ways of looking at practical problems and consequently go about their business in a more clear-headed and informed manner. With the coming of the BEd in the fourth year, however, there is no reason why a beginning should not be made with the other task of training specialists in the relevant branches of educational theory who may later come to hold responsible positions in Colleges and Schools. But we must constantly be on our guard that this is not done in such a way that the orientation of the three year course becomes less down-to-earth and less concerned with the concrete problems of teaching children.

5   The influence of theory on practice

Perhaps my approach to these matters may seem to you somewhat perverse and paradoxical. Here am I, who have spent most of my professional life as a philosopher — yet I seem to be constantly stressing the practical; I am also now an 'education' rather than a 'subject' specialist — yet I seem to accord priority to the mastery of 'subjects' in teacher training. How can I justify these emphases? The emphasis on 'subjects' is not difficult to justify. For it is a matter of logical necessity that a teacher must have something to teach. This conclusion is secure at least if we want to build on a rock-bottom foundation in determining what counts as a specific preparation for teaching. When we rise from this into the realm of general theory of education we are dealing with much more speculative matters.

The research on these matters collected together by Wallen and Travers in their 'Analysis and Investigation of Teaching Methods' in N. L. Gage, *Handbook of Research on Teaching* (Rand McNally, Chicago, 1963) may make depressing reading for any educational theorist. The theme that runs through the article is that of the lack of evidence supporting many of our cherished convictions about the effect of theory on practice. There is evidence all right that the student develops an affective response towards a number of ideas related to education, and that these affective responses come to be supported by a cognitive structure. But there is little evidence to suggest that these ideas become translated into action-systems through which the results of teacher training may be manifested in the class-room. Many teacher-training programmes, for instance, concentrate on giving a deep and extensive understanding of children and their development. But 'The little evidence available at present suggests that most teachers have relatively little understanding of their pupils and that

161

differences in understanding which occur from one teacher to another have little effect on the learning process' (p. 458). The effect of training programmes on the practice of teachers in class-rooms is nugatory compared with the influence of models in their past with whom they identify and of demands springing from their own personalities. The teacher, for instance, who is never happy unless he has some highly structured, formal situation in which he can talk in an uninterrupted fashion, is not likely to be practising a method that has the blessing of his College or the support of a volume of research findings. He is much more likely to be responding to some inner need or copying some early exemplar. It is depressing to find, too, how little evidence psychology has, in fact, provided for methods which are advocated with a fervour more appropriate to religious causes. Even more depressing is the speed with which educationalists have embraced psychological theories which seem vaguely to support convictions derived from other sources — for instance the widespread acceptance of Gestalt psychology by those who were advocates of 'wholeness', or the popularity of Piaget amongst those who are convinced of the importance of do-it-yourself methods. How rarely does one find educational theorists following the elementary advice dating back to Francis Bacon that we should look for the negative instance, that we should consciously look for counter-examples to refute our cherished theories? But as Bacon pointed out, this emphasis on falsification, which is the kernel of the scientific method, goes against our inveterate tendency to believe what we wish to be true. Educationalists in the grip of an ideology are particularly prone to this common human failing.

If we were bent on bringing to bear some fairly solid influence on practice during teacher training we might be wise to experiment much more radically with the systematic apprenticeship of students to experienced teachers whose practices had been shown to be effective. General considerations about the imparting of ways of behaving adduced by Oakeshott in his 'Political Education'[1] and 'Teaching and Learning'[2] would support these hints from research. For how to organize a situation efficiently so that many children can learn, either individually or as a class, is such a complicated skill that it could not possibly be learnt without plenty of practice on the spot. If this practice is not modelled on that of some current exemplar, the overwhelming likelihood is that the teacher will revert to some earlier exemplar. For no one could begin to teach without identifying to a certain extent with someone from whom the practices could be picked up. And the exemplars which would probably exert this hidden influence are likely to be a mixed bag, to put it mildly. In the nature of the case, too, they are unlikely to be those who were adept at methods appropriate to the primary stage of education.

To pursue this matter further would involve us in complicated matters to do with the organization of teaching practice. My conviction is that we should move towards a much closer co-operation with schools, involving the use of what in the USA they call 'master teachers', in ways that seem desirable to us. My fear is that, if we do not do this, we shall be forced into doing it in ways that may prove to be highly undesirable!

The fact, however, that there is little evidence for the immediate influence of theory on practice should not unduly depress us. For I would never have expected there to be any such sudden transformation. For teaching is not a technology in which theoretical findings can be immediately fed in to practice and applied in any simple straightforward way. There are, of course, some things of an elementary sort that fall into this category, such as the use of rest-pauses, incentives, and practices. But most of teaching involves a highly subtle moralized interrelationship between persons which cannot be reduced to a collection of techniques without debasing the relationships involved and making them less than personal. The effect of theory should therefore be long-term — the gradual transformation of a person's view of children, of himself, and of the situation in which he is acting. Not long ago we had a visiting professor of education who sat in on some of the seminars in our department to study what we were doing. At the end of a seminar on morals he asked the students what difference their evening's deliberations would make to how they dealt with the children they had to face on the following morning. They cooked up a few bright remarks to satisfy his sensitivities, but what they said to each other after he had gone was that if he had been through the course he would not have asked such a damn silly question! But they were experienced teachers who had, as it were, come back because they felt the need for more theory. I doubt if students at the level of initial training would have reacted like this. And so we return to the role of theory during initial training.

In my view the main function of educational theory at this stage should be to remove certain naiveties that students bring to the educational situation, through having only participated in it at the consumer end, and gradually to restructure their view of the situation in which they have to act. It should sensitize their awareness of what they are doing so that they will not despise it or be impatient with it, but develop a determination to get down to it properly at a later stage when they have had enough experience for it to be fully meaningful to them. I stress the approach to educational theory via practical problems partly because this reflects my own view of the nature of educational theory and partly because I think that this type of approach is more likely than any other approach to stimulate students to think more about what they are doing.

The traditional approach to teacher training has been to supplement a basic training in subjects and the handing on of skills by an attempt to bring about commitment to some sort of ideology. The ideology was conveyed by what is often called 'Principles of Education' backed up by a smattering of the right sort of psychology. This was peculiarly appropriate to small single-sex Colleges staffed largely by dedicated women. The time for this is now passing. Colleges are getting much larger and mixed; there are problems of discipline and consensus; and all sorts of new ideas are flowing into them. The educational system of the country is in a highly fluid state; there is little agreement about aims of education; the curriculum is everywhere under discussion; teaching methods are constantly being queried and the lack of established knowledge about their effectiveness is becoming patent to any serious student of education.

In a situation like this any cosy ideology is not only an

irrelevance; it can also positively hamstring a teacher. I heard of a case a few weeks ago where a student dutifully set up an interest table in one of our tougher types of London school. The children calmly swiped the lot. The supervisor complained to the head who remarked that he had put the student in the best behaved class in the school and that the children in this school were not ready for those sorts of methods. 'But I cannot give up my principles' protested the lecturer. But *Half Our Future* has a past which renders them initially unresponsive to methods more suitable to children emerging from middle-class homes, which provide not only plenty of language and materials, but also attitudes favourable to learning and a system of social control that is responsive to individual differences. If we are going to be child-centred, for heaven's sake let us actually study the children whom we have to teach. Bernstein's work suggests that in the case of socially disadvantaged children in our Infant schools the teacher may need to control and plan the cognitive, linguistic, and social explorations of the child more than in the case of privileged children. There is also the problem created by the shortage of places in schools for teaching practice. Students are now having increasingly to do their practices in the sorts of schools in which they may later have to teach!

The moral of all this is not, of course, that we should throw overboard all that has been learnt from 'progressive' methods and revert to archaic systems of undiluted mass instruction. It is rather that we should do all in our power to help teachers to develop a critical, empirical, adaptable attitude to methods of teaching, and encourage them to learn to think on their feet and experiment with different ways of teaching different types of subjects to different types of children. We should regard it as a blot on a College if a student's first concern on teaching practice is to discover *the* method approved of by her supervisor, for fear of being marked down if she tries something on her own. We should also regard it as a blot if we hear, as we too often *do* hear, a sensible remark prefaced by the phrase 'Though I scarcely dare say it within the walls of my College. . . .' What are Colleges of Education? Centres of indoctrination, or places where students — and staff for that matter — can learn to think fearlessly for themselves? If only this critical, experimental attitude to teaching could be more encouraged we might soon cease to turn out teachers who thought that if they can only keep talking — or stop talking — then children are necessarily learning something, or teachers who practise something approximating to a free day without keeping a careful check on what in fact each child has learnt. Better still, we might turn out no teachers for whom 'teaching' has become a dirty word.

The development of a critical, independent, experimental approach to problems of teaching is a lengthy business. It is an exercise in education, not in any narrowly conceived system of training. If students go out from our Colleges with at least the rudiments of this they will have as 'specific' a preparation for teaching under modern conditions as any course in 'education' can provide at the level of initial training. They may even begin to tell us that their course in educational theory is as valuable a part of their training as their study of subjects and their teaching practice!

Notes

1 In M. Oakeshott, *Rationalism in Politics*, London, Methuen, 1968.
2 In R. S. Peters (ed.), *The Concept of Education*, London, Routledge & Kegan Paul, 1967.

Education as an academic discipline

I take, as my starting point, that education, as a subject, is like politics in being concerned with problems which cannot be tackled, like mathematical problems or problems in physics, by reliance on just one way of thinking. Educational problems are problems such as 'Ought we to have corporal punishment in a secondary school?' or 'Does learning improve as a result of an integrated curriculum?' or 'Should nursery education be expanded?' We cannot, or should not, devise empirical studies to help us tackle such questions until we have, first of all, done some work on concepts such as 'punishment', 'integration' and 'education'. We have to distinguish punishment from discipline and from the sorts of things that psychologists do to dogs when they subject them to negative reinforcement. We have to enquire into the difference between 'integration' and 'interdisciplinary' studies, strong and weak senses of 'integration' and so on. We have to distinguish 'education' from 'socialization'. In these three illustrative examples we have also to raise questions about the justification of punishment, the status of differentiated ways of knowing and the interplay between educational and economic arguments. Only then are we in a fit position to see what sorts of empirical studies are relevant, whether they are psychological or sociological in form. Investigations into the effects of punishment on offenders, for instance, will only be decisive if a particular ethical position is adopted about the reasons for punishing people in general and children in particular. This structuring of the situation for investigation is not, as many claim or fear, just the business of the philosopher. Psychologists and sociologists, as well as historians, have much to say that is relevant to the application of concepts such as 'punishment', 'integration' and 'education'. For they shift in varying social situations, periods of history, and stages of children's development. Social and developmental variables affect, too, the relevance of reasons which can be given for educational policies and practices.

Given that educational studies have this interdisciplinary character, is there any reason why they should not be ranked as a respectable academic 'discipline'? Obviously they do not constitute a discipline if by 'discipline' we mean a form of learning that is structured in terms of a single type of truth-criterion and a determinate methodology that is derivative from it. For, in this sense, as I have already argued, educational studies comprise a meeting point of such 'disciplines' in relation to a collection of concrete problems. But this does not constitute a sufficient reason for excluding them from academic institutions, unless politics, law and economics are to be excluded, especially as their contributing foundation disciplines — i.e. philosophy, psychology, history and sociology — are already well-established in academic institutions. Indeed, at a time when there is a general outcry against the fragmentation and compartmentalization of knowledge, and when attempts are made, often of a highly artificial sort, to 'integrate' various disciplines, a subject like that of educational studies, which is interdisciplinary by its very nature, should surely be welcomed.

Is, then, the problem-centred character of educational studies incompatible with its being an 'academic' subject? Presumably the question at issue is whether or not educational studies must be concerned with practical problems rather than with those which are studied in a more reflective, disinterested manner, whatever value one places on 'academic' if it is used in this sense. The answer to this is that, though most people study education as a subject with practical concerns in view, it need not necessarily be so studied. For it can be concerned with concrete problems of a theoretical sort as well as with practical problems at a high level of generality. Just as in the study of politics a scholar can be consumed with curiosity about how far political decisions are influenced by the advice of civil servants, without ever wanting to deal with a civil servant or to influence a politician, so too can a student of education be consumed with curiosity about how attainment at school is related to socio-economic background without having any burning concern to improve

attainment. Or he might just wonder whether comprehensiva-
tion is a desirable policy for secondary education without
being particularly concerned to influence events. In this
respect the study of education is like the study of medicine
or engineering with which it is so often compared. I myself
would find it difficult, working in an applied field of
philosophy, to take such a detached stance. But those who
do, have a defensible position.

Why, then, the traditional hostility towards education as a
field of study in an academic institution such as a university?
Perhaps because it is, unlike law and medicine, connected
with a low-status profession whose members are very numerous. Perhaps because it is also a subject about which all
academics think they know something because of their practical experience of teaching. But also, surely, because at least
three phases of the development of educational studies can
be distinguished and the standard reaction of academics to
them is determined largely by encounters with their exponents during its first phase. This was the phase of what I once
called the 'undifferentiated mush' of educational theory. It
was not, actually, altogether undifferentiated; for a rather
woolly sort of wisdom was often backed up by a certain
amount of more precise information from psychology and
from the history of education.

In the 1960s it became appreciated that philosophy, in the
professional philosopher's sense of 'philosophy', had much to
contribute as well as sociology. So the second phase of the
differentiated approach to educational problems developed
with altogether predictable results. The contributing disciplines went their way with some success but at a cost to educational theory as a whole; for their representatives became
increasingly incapable of talking to each other. This was in
part due to a widespread and mistaken identification of the
logic of the subject to be taught with its pedagogy. By that
I mean that, because it became appreciated that educational
problems require differentiated forms of thinking for their
solution, it was assumed that education as a subject should
be taught mainly by training people in the relevant disciplines
in isolation from each other. The students, it was often said,
will make their own 'integration' of what they have learnt in

169

the contributing disciplines. But how many have in fact done so? And surely thought about educational problems requires learning situations in which an attempt is made to integrate the different approaches in relation to concrete problems as well as learning situations in which specific aspects of problems are pursued in the distinct disciplines. To what extent learning situations should be differentiated or integrated depends very much on the problems concerned, the level of the students, the availability of tutors and so on. There is no room for dogmatism about this at the present stage of our ignorance. But because of the new emphasis on differentiation at this second stage of the development of educational theory, the net result was that questions such as 'Ought we to use corporal punishment?' remained unanswered because people working in the philosophy of punishment became either institutionally or intellectually separated from those who were tackling the psychological or historical aspects of the problem. Or perhaps, a great deal of work was done by philosophers in a given area but no corresponding work by representatives of other disciplines. The third phase of educational theory, the attempt to integrate these contributing disciplines round concrete problems, is now beginning.

An obstacle to this development has been another entirely predictable tendency, which is for those who have immersed themselves in the contributing disciplines to become increasingly absorbed by more general issues in these disciplines and to find their interest fading in the more messy, mundane sphere of educational application. Just as in the old heyday of the dominance of behaviourism in psychology many thought that a man could only retain his integrity as a psychologist contributing to education if he worked heroically at extrapolating fragments of drive-reduction or stimulus-response psychology to the class-room, so also those delving in philosophy have thought that philosophy consists in something called 'conceptual analysis' and *all* that the philosopher can do is to enter the ring in search for some conceptual promontory of the body of educational discourse which he can get a critical hold on with his half-nelson. Dewey provided a much more promising paradigm. He insisted that thought, about education or anything else, must start from problems.

Unfortunately he had too stereotyped a view of the mould into which problems must be cast.

Another obstacle to the actual tackling of educational problems has been the understandable aggression of an insecure discipline trying to establish itself, obtain timetable space for teaching, and staff to carry the teaching load. It must be admitted, for instance, that philosophy of education put itself on the map, to a certain extent, by attacking some of the woolly panaceas of progressive education. Its exponents have not always attempted to discern the view of life and of education which lies behind exuberant hosannas such as 'Let the children grow'. There has, too often, been a confrontation of talk rather than a meeting of minds. Similarly sociology of education has recently launched into tirades about the organization of knowledge. In developing a generalized and fashionable anti-establishment line it has often ignored the crucial distinction between the social basis of knowledge itself and of the ways of transmitting knowledge, and has proceeded in sublime ignorance of centuries of work in epistemology on problems of truth and objectivity. It has generalized about historical conditions without exhibiting any detailed knowledge of history. And, perhaps, in this general struggle for recognition, the historians have shown too little aggression. They have worked soberly, if sleepily, away at problems without blinking an eye-lid at extravagant utterances about, for instance, the development of child-centred education or the historical determinants of the curriculum.

Mention of the curriculum introduces another aspect of the recent development of education as an academic discipline. 'Curriculum' is now, of course, the with-it concept that tends to be stuck like a label on many band-waggons in spite of the obscurity surrounding what is covered by the term 'curriculum'. In the old days education itself used to have aims, content and methods. 'Curriculum' was a very vague word referring roughly to what was taught explicitly, to content if you like. Nowadays, however, it is thought itself to encompass objectives (preferably measurable 'behavioural' ones), content and methods. There is also a hidden curriculum. But, leaving aside these conceptual niceties, curriculum studies have in fact proved to be an area in which there *has*

171

been co-operation between representatives of foundation disciplines and between them and specialists in school-subjects and age ranges. In my view the most productive results have come about when, as in Nuffield science and classics, there has been co-operation between specialists in the subject concerned and some foundation discipline such as developmental psychology. I have a horror of generalized talk about the curriculum by those who know little of the problems connected with teaching particular subjects. It reminds me of specialists in 'teaching methods' who mutter darkly, after being closeted briefly with members of the Faculty of Arts, that 'arts subjects' present peculiar difficulties. As if, on the one hand, that they might not; and as if, on the other hand, that the difficulties of teaching French had much in common with those of teaching philosophy or history.

A criticism, perhaps, of curriculum studies is that they do not go far enough in involving foundation disciplines other than psychology from the start. There is much to be learnt in the sociology of education, for instance, about the influence of organizational factors on the transmission and sharing of understanding. It is amazing that many practitioners of the new mathematics do not realize that a distinctive and arguable position within the philosophy of mathematics is presupposed by their approach. It is regrettable, too, that so few joint appointments are made in universities between other departments and the education department — e.g. a lecturer in the mathematics department who teaches mathematics to undergraduates and who also specializes, in association with the education department, in problems to do with the teaching of mathematics, from which his colleagues in the mathematics department might also benefit. Actually it is this sphere of educational studies that one often has difficulty in persuading fellow academics to take seriously. They are prepared to concede that there is work to be done in philosophy of education and educational psychology if this is confined to general problems of teaching, learning, motivation, freedom, authority, discipline and so on. But they do not appreciate the complexities introduced by the fact that education, in so far as it necessarily involves learning, requires a two-tiered type of academic study. For there is always a variable content which itself constitutes an academic study as well as forms and conditions of learning and teaching which also require foundation studies of an academic type. These colleagues themselves are usually authorities on the content to be learnt, and, of course, the manner of learning is in part determined by the character of this content. But not entirely; for one of the crucial questions in this field is the extent to which methods of learning are determined by the content of what has to be learnt. And it is very difficult to distinguish logical from psychological questions about learning. The intellectual difficulties underlying these issues are expressed at an institutional level in conflicts and insecurities about who is to determine the manner of learning and teaching. Should it be decided by subject specialists with an interest in the child development, learning and motivation? In Colleges of Education conflicts between lecturers and main subject lecturers over what are called 'curriculum courses' reflect these intellectual perplexities.

It is easy to understand, in the light of this brief analysis, how university teachers are likely to react to problems about the curriculum. Because of their detailed knowledge of the content of their subjects they will tend to think all that is required is that school-teachers should acquire from them a detailed grasp of the content of a subject, together with a few practical tips about how to put it over to children at different levels in a school. They will tend to think, perhaps, that the logic of the subject should determine the way in which it is presented to children. They will, therefore, view with impatience the views of those who are interested in child development and the psychology of learning, and make sharp comments about the overriding importance of the teacher having a thorough knowledge of what is taught. And, of course, they are partly right. But they are wrong in erecting a necessary condition of good teaching into a sufficient condition. *A fortiori* they may tend to resent suggestions from educational theorists about how they might improve the teaching of their own subjects.

Is the development of curriculum theory, then, a paradigm for the third phase of development of education as an academic study? Not, of course, if we think that we can proceed by some rational stereotype of getting clear, in any problem area, what our objectives are — a phase in which philosophers are meant to be of some use; then calling in psychologists and sociologists to design experiments for possible ways of attaining these objectives; and then, finally, calling in the testers to evaluate success. For philosophers, historians and sociologists alike would indicate the flaws in this rationalist bed-rock. It would only serve as a useful paradigm if we are prepared to start from problems with less confidence about what they are and how they can be tackled — if indeed they are just problems rather than predicaments.

To start with, I would hope this area of problems should make us pause if we are confident about the division of labour in tackling them. A curriculum involves people learning things in which knowledge and understanding occupy a prominent position. But who is clear what the psychology of learning and thinking are as distinct from philosophical questions about them? When I first read Bruner's *The Process of Education* a vague feeling of familiarity came over me. Where had I read this sort of stuff before? And then I remembered. It was in Mill's *System of Logic*, or in Whewell, or someone like that. Then there is Piaget churning out all those works in what he considers epistemology. But his work is taken as a series of psychological texts. Modern philosophers stress that concepts can only be understood in the context of a form of social life, much of which is non-linguistic. And then they find sociologists of education going to town on this as a new discovery in sociology. And how much of the efficacy of programme-learning depends upon psychological generalizations about learning, and how much on the detailed study of those who know about the subjects to be learnt, which enables them to break down the subject matter into small incremental steps? Are we so clear about the borderlines of our contributing disciplines that we can behave like shop stewards over demarcation disputes?

I am convinced that curriculum projects would benefit if people representing different perspectives on educational problems were involved constructively in devising them instead of shooting them down after they have got off the ground. How many of those planning such projects, for instance, have uncritically started from some version of Bloom's taxonomy? And how much time has been spent by others in later exposing its inadequacies, which vitiated the whole enterprise from the start? If philosophers spent less time in exposing the conceptual confusions of others, and sociologists less time in diagnosing other people's social stances, and both spent more time constructively in getting in on the ground floor of the investigation of concrete educational problems, educational theory would gain enormously. The point is that these sorts of critique do not appear very helpful if made from without and at an advanced stage in a project. One hears, for instance, of comments being invited but completely disregarded when they turn out to be radically critical. But if they had been made from the inside and at an earlier stage they might have made some difference.

Or is it the case that some people are so confident about what our problems are and how they can be solved that they can adopt a cavalier attitude to cogent criticism? I hope not; for in my opinion our state of ignorance with regard to teaching and learning is about comparable to that of the Greeks with regard to medicine or meteorology. Many of the arguments between progressives and traditionalists with regard to teaching methods, for instance, resemble the old fights about creeds. But we now quote small-scale favourable pieces of research instead of texts, and we sometimes decide issues by committee confrontations instead of by clubs. The hope is that more coal-face co-operation between representatives of different disciplines would do something towards dissipating more generalized tensions between the disciplines. We tend to see those in other disciplines through spectacles coloured by our own insecurities. If you are not a philosopher you may well believe that there is something called conceptual analysis, to which philosophers necessarily subscribe, which is closely connected with a fixated, Burkian type of view of ordinary language. If you are not a sociologist you may believe that sociologists necessarily subscribe to either Marxism or ethno-methodology; if you are not a psychologist you may well believe that psychologists are either behaviourists, or Freudians, or plodders on the Piagetian path. But systematic co-operation on a concrete problem sometimes dents these facile sterotypes.

175

The other type of case for co-operation on concrete issues is as valid for work in the contributing disciplines themselves as for work of a more interdisciplinary sort. It concerns the distinctiveness of work deriving from the 'pure' disciplines when they are applied in the educational sphere. This raises the much misused notion of 'relevance'. Without embarking on the difficulties of this over-worked notion at least two points can be made about the 'relevance' of theory to practice. It can be thought of as being relevant in **some** immediate sense, in the way in which a knowledge of chemistry can be used to blow up a building or to melt some ice. Educational theory may be fed into the solution of a limited number of educational problems in a similar way — e.g. in the teaching of skills. But 'relevance' is more often of a more generalized sort. It is usual, but mistaken, to make a sharp distinction between thought and action, between behaviour and consciousness. This will not do, because actions are identified basically by the conceptions and purposes of those who perform them, just as different forms of behaviour are inseparable from the view of a situation of the person behaving. Now, if exposure to theory is conducted so that it is not just learnt up as a collection of inert ideas, a person's outlook will gradually be transformed by it. He will view a classroom situation, for instance, in a very different light; he will have a different view of what is problematic about it, and the sort of thing that needs to be done to improve it.

If one starts from a concrete issue in education, therefore — for instance a problem about the role of the head, about pupil participation, or about punishment — how far does one have to go into the type of thought provided by the discipline concerned? From the point of view of educational theory one has to bear in mind some maxim such as 'If it doesn't itch, don't scratch'. By that I mean that one has to go as far as necessary for tackling the particular problem. But one cannot tell in advance how far that is. I do know, however, that in supervising people's PhDs I constantly have to say something like 'These are interesting philosophical points; but what light do they throw on the educational problem from which you started?' I also know that some philosophers of education have proceeded in exactly the opposite way. They have done some philosophy in a way approved by their colleagues in the philosophy department, just as psychologists have done psychology according to some paradigm of what is thought 'scientific'; they have then scratched their heads and have asked: 'What is the relevance of this to what goes on in schools and class-rooms?' This represents the other extreme. Of course it *might* be relevant. For instance, whether you can call Piaget's work philosophy or psychology, it is certainly very relevant to problems of teaching and learning. But he did not do it with any practical educational problems in mind. It is not, therefore, necessarily the intentions of the author of some particular piece of theory which are crucial, so much as the connexion of the final product with some educational problem. It is this connecting thread which gives educational theory whatever unity it possesses.

What is the upshot of these rambling remarks for education as an academic study? Does it imply that we should abandon the differentiated approach? In my view, certainly not; rather we should plan more cautiously for combining a differentiated approach with more careful interdisciplinary, problem-centred work. To give you a recent example which I witnessed of what we must avoid: I recently attended a conference organized by philosophers of education at which there was also a good sprinkling of psychologists and pure philosophers. One paper was on 'Discovery methods'. An attempt was being made to follow up Kohlberg's suggestion that conditions of learning should resemble Socrates' session with the slave in *Meno*. The paper met with a pretty critical reception. The philosophers soon brought out that the speaker's thoughts about Plato were pretty superficial and impressionistic; the psychologists were aghast at the misunderstandings of Piaget and Bruner. And those present who had actually used discovery methods in teaching maintained that he did not give a recognizable account of their practice. So the paper satisfied nobody who had precise knowledge of the areas from which he was drawing in order to develop his thesis. But, for all that, the paper was well conceived as an attempt to explore an educational problem.

The next phase of education as a subject, as I see it, is to provide contexts of research and teaching which enable this sort of enterprise to be conducted in a more competent

177

manner. To make this practicable, education lecturers must live somehow in three worlds at once. To use the Freudian imagery, they must have a super-ego and id as well as an ego. Their ego, or centre of identity, must presumably be in the educational aspect of the form of understanding in which they have specialized. This might be philosophy of education or it might be the teaching of history. This is their bread and butter world. But they must not lose touch with the voice of the father, with their super-ego. And this means, in the cases which I have used as examples, they must keep abreast with what is going on in the pure discipline. And this means literally not losing touch with their father. There is nothing worse than the way in which members of some education departments in universities are both physically and psychologically isolated from those in the same university who are working in the pure disciplines. This is one of the great weaknesses of what might be referred to, in a kind of shorthand, as the North American situation of the School of Education. Then there is the id — a slight misnomer, actually. By this I mean the more adventurous, insecure, unfettered venturing forth to explore problems with others whose approach may seem alien — a world simmering with repressed aggression and with the anxieties of an unstructured situation. But it is precisely in this area that we have to establish some kind of *collective* identity as workers in educational theory. We have it all right as far as our ego is concerned. Some of us work at keeping on terms with our super-ego; we try not to let it be just a voice from a very distant past. But, for lack of understanding, we feel powerless when we contemplate doing what we deeply yearn to do, namely actually putting forward an answer to an educational problem. How can we do this in a way which satisfies both our ego and that of our colleagues who have a different perspective on the problem concerned?

I would suggest that one way of tackling it is to venture forth in a piecemeal way and to form either a research or a teaching group with others in relation to some particular problem or area of interest, e.g. discovery methods, moral education, examinations, etc. We might have to pick our colleagues very carefully — and not just for personal reasons; for some types of approach within the contributing disciplines might be completely incompatible with our own. Or — tell it not in Gath — we might just decide to do it ourselves. This, actually, sometimes occasions acute anxieties, believe it or not. Before I came to the Institute I held a joint appointment at Birkbeck in the philosophy and psychology departments. When I had been at the Institute some time I was asked to take part in a joint symposium of an interdisciplinary kind on moral development. I said that I could manage both the philosophical and the psychological aspects of this topic but would need the help of a sympathetic sociologist. The roof nearly went off the place. The philosopher was making a takeover bid; the psychologist was being done out of his rights, etc.! How absurd can we get? It would, of course, be absurd to suggest that on *any* topic a person trained in philosophy could do justice to the psychology; but surely this sort of thing would be manageable in a *few* areas of abiding interest to him. Indeed I would put the matter more strongly: I would say that educational theory *proper* will only be developed if individuals or groups of like-minded people launch forth and start doing this. I had a most exhilarating summer in a small Education Department in a university in New Zealand — in my view one of the best in Australasia. There was only one other philosopher of education on the staff but two extremely good educational psychologists. I spent hours of time discussing educational problems with them and pouring over massive tomes of child development. There were no demarcation disputes or worries about who was doing what. We just had a go at problems. This department, however, was, as most departments of education are in New Zealand, an outpost of the Scottish system. They trained no teachers. The staff-room, therefore, did not buzz with concrete problems encountered in schools. Indeed the whole issue of contact with schools presented difficulties. Furthermore there was a complete absence of methods people on the staff. A whole dimension of the situation of education as an academic study was missing.

This is the other sphere for the launching of limited co-operative projects, that of co-operation not just between those responsible for teaching different methods subjects, but between methods people and foundation specialists. In philosophy itself there are a whole range of philosophies of — e.g.

179

philosophy of science, mathematics, history, religion, language, as well as aesthetics. Only in some cases — e.g. the philosophy of history, has there been a lot of disciplined thought about the nature of the subject in relation to how the subject should be taught. For various reasons philosophy of education has concentrated more on general educational issues rather than on those connected with particular forms of learning. The same, surely, is true of theories of learning and motivation in psychology. There is limitless scope for co-operative projects in these areas.

Perhaps, too, the time is ripe for us to return with rather more discriminating eyes towards some of our great precursors in educational theory. We now shudder at the Cook's tour method of treating some of the great educators. But if we studied some of the really competent ones such as Herbart, William James, Durkheim and Plato and took a closer look at how they wove together the different strands of educational theory in their systems in relation to problems — ethics, psychology, theory of knowledge, sociology and so on — this might prove very rewarding, not just as a way of looking at ourselves and what we are doing a bit more coherently and critically, but also as helping us to assimilate some of the wilder ravings of our ids into a less circumscribed and bounded ego. It might help us, in other words, towards establishing a more coherent type of identity for lecturers in education. I am not saying, of course, that such an approach to some of the great educators should be introduced in a one year course of initial training. There are problems of priority and it would be difficult to do justice to such a study in a brief problem-centred course which includes at least twelve weeks of teaching practice. An advanced course or a three-year degree course in educational studies would be a much more appropriate place. But I do feel that the time is ripe for a new look at some of the theorists in the past who did not just enthuse in an amateurish way about ideas thrown up by successful practices, but who attempted to tackle systematically educational problems in the light of what was then known in the contributing disciplines. In educational studies we tend to be somewhat embarrassed by our recent past, but we should not forget that we also have a more disciplined history.

The role and responsibilities of the university in teacher education

10

At the moment the teaching profession seems to be rising up in arms against the suggestion, emanating from an inspired leak from the James Committee, that the link between universities and colleges of education should be weakened, if not severed altogether. The colleges, it is rumoured, are to be relegated to a kind of secondary modern area of higher education and given an inferior type of degree. Better, it is argued, a real degree like the BEd for some than a kind of academic green-label stamp for all.

These arguments about status are extremely important; for neglect of such obvious considerations was one of the reasons which led to the abortiveness of the ill-fated secondary modern schools. This down-grading of the profession will obviously have an immediate effect on recruitment to the profession and, hence, a long-term effect on the quality of education in schools. I do not, however, in this article propose to dwell on these wider social issues. I want to concentrate on the educational reasons for preserving and strengthening the link between the universities and the teaching profession. Everything in the garden is not lovely, as everybody involved in the business of the education of teachers knows too well. But there is danger in mistaking a temporary phase in growth for a permanent condition. And all is not so ill with it that it obviously requires uprooting and a new start in the local authority's recreation ground.

What, then, are the basic reasons why the teaching profession, like the legal or medical profession, should be closely associated with universities? To answer this question something must be said about the nature of a university as an institution. Its relation to the teaching profession can then be explored.

181

The university as an institution

Institutions are not entities like toads or trees; they are constituted largely by the conceptions of men. Individuals, of
course, may have idiosyncratic purposes for becoming members of an institution. Men may join the police force, for
instance, for the pay, prestige or opportunities for domination which it offers; but in so far as they are policemen they
must conceive of themselves, to a certain extent, as concerned with the preservation of law and order. This dominant
aim provides a unitary thread to their lives which persists
through time.

University teachers conceive of themselves as concerned
mainly with the advancement of understanding and with the
initiation of others into it. This is an aim which is dominant
in our present conception of a university. By many this aim
of the advancement of knowledge is interpreted in terms of
disinterested research. But this emphasis is a modern one.
Traditionally the university has been thought of as concerned
equally with the development of knowledge that can be
applied to the practical needs of the community and with the
training of people for the professions — e.g. of medicine and
law. The assumption has been that certain professions require such an underpinning in theory. Doctors have been
trained in universities but not cavalry officers. Another aim,
too, has traditionally been very important — the provision of
opportunities for liberal education, in the sense of the
development of all-round understanding which is relevant to
the personal development of students. In our conception of a
university at least these three aims are intertwined, though at
the moment the emphasis on pure research may be dominant. If, for instance, an institution devoted itself entirely to
the development of applied knowledge and training for
industry and the professions, I think we would tend to think
that it was really an institute of technology. If it devoted
itself entirely to liberal education, without any emphasis on
research, I think we would say that the institution was a
liberal arts college. But equally, if it devoted itself purely to
research, and to the training of people in it, I think we
would say that it had become a graduate school.

182

To say that the promotion of one of these aims is the 'essence' of a university would be to tighten up the concept in a certain direction, though it is conceivable that this might happen; for, as I started by saying, institutions are constituted largely by the conceptions of men, and if university teachers as a whole conceived of themselves as concerned only with the development of pure research, universities might in fact come to have this essence. The only really strong argument for insisting on such an essence for a university would be one which showed that pure research could not be carried on properly in an institution which was concerned also with applied knowledge and with the general education of students. Universities such as Oxford would, I think, be standing refutations of this sweeping claim. I shall assume, therefore, that all three types of aims are legitimate ones for a university and that what is distinctive of a university as distinct from a graduate school, an institute of technology and a liberal arts college, is that it tries to pursue all three of them at the same time. Different universities put rather different emphasis on these different but related aims.

Should universities be concerned with educational studies?

What, then, is distinctive about educational studies and should universities concern themselves with them? The trouble about educational studies, which, in part, explains the traditional hostility of universities towards them is that, logically speaking, they are a mess and necessarily a mess. By this I mean that they are concerned with problems which cannot be tackled, like mathematical problems or problems in physics, by reliance on just one way of thinking. Educational problems are problems such as 'Ought we to punish children?' or 'Should classes be streamed?' or 'Should we have an integrated curriculum?' We cannot devise experiments to help us tackle such questions until we have, first of all, done some philosophical work on concepts such as 'punishment' and 'integration'. We have to distinguish 'punishment' from 'discipline' and from what psychologists do to rats and dogs when they give them negative reinforcement. We then

183

have to raise questions about the justification of punishment, the aims of education, and moral principles underlying human relations. Only then are we in a fit position to see what sorts of empirical studies are relevant, whether they are psychological or sociological in form.

At least three phases in the development of educational theory can be distinguished which are very relevant to how it should be conceived as a university study. Much of the hostility towards educational theory derives, I think, from the fact that most university teachers are familiar mainly with the first phase of it. This is the phase of what I once called 'undifferentiated mush'. A rather woolly sort of wisdom was dispensed as answers to these complex questions, backed up by a certain amount of more precise information from psychology and from the history of education. Early in the 1960s the second phase got off the ground. It was appreciated that philosophy, in the professional philosopher's sense of 'philosophy', had much to contribute to these problems, as well as sociology. The differentiated approach to educational problems began to develop in a more explicit way, with an altogether predictable result. It was now found that the contributory disciplines were going their own way with some success but at a cost to educational theory. Their representatives were becoming increasingly incapable of talking to each other. The net result was that questions such as 'Ought we to punish children?' remained unanswered because the people working on the philosophy of punishment became either institutionally or intellectually separated from those who were dealing with the psychological or sociological aspects of this problem. Or, perhaps, a great deal of work was done by philosophers in a given area and no corresponding work by representatives of other disciplines. The third phase of educational theory is now beginning to develop. Attempts are being made to bring people from the different disciplines together in relation to practical problems, and to train them in more than one specialized way of thinking about these problems.

'Integration', however, is not just a matter of drawing together what are often called 'foundation disciplines' in educational theory, such as philosophy, psychology, sociology and history, and relating them to practical problems; it is also very much concerned with what are called 'curriculum studies'. 'Curriculum' is now, of course, the with-it concept that tends to be stuck like a label on numerous band-waggons. In the old days education used to have aims, content, and methods. 'Curriculum' used to be a very vague word for referring to what was explicitly taught — to content, if you like. Nowadays, however, the curriculum itself is thought to include objectives (preferably measurable ones), content, and methods. But, leaving aside this conceptual shift, a very obvious point about 'education' is that it suggests that *something* is being learnt. The manner of learning, too, will be, in part, determined by what is being learnt. As soon as questions of content are raised all the subjects come to mind with which university teachers themselves are concerned, as well as difficult questions about subject boundaries, 'integration' and the relations between 'subjects' and 'forms of thought' which are two different ways of looking at this content. Making this type of distinction is only a start in tackling very difficult questions about the logical structure of these subjects and their relation to others. But if these subjects are to be *taught*, especially at the school level, additional questions about the psychology of learning become relevant, with attendant difficulties and obscurities; for it is very difficult to distinguish logical from psychological questions about learning. And the intellectual difficulties underlying these issues are expressed at an institutional level in conflicts and insecurities about who is to determine the manner of learning and teaching. Should it be decided by subject specialists with an interest in the philosophy of their subject? Or should it be psychologists with an interest in child development, learning, and motivation? In colleges of education conflicts between Education lecturers and main subject lecturers over what are called 'curriculum courses' reflect these intellectual perplexities.

How would educational studies so conceived fit into the conception of a university which has been outlined? Eminently well, I would say. First of all, although educational problems, like political ones, are practical in character, attempts to deal with them can be the subject for disinterested study by people who are not actively engaged in the solution of such problems. So even a purist amongst university teachers, who thinks that universities should only be concerned with the disinterested pursuit of knowledge, has on this count no more reason for excluding educational studies than he has for excluding political studies.

Neither could doubts be entertained about educational studies of the sort that might be entertained about cosmetology, which, it might be argued, does not rely enough on fundamental research to be a university study; for the problem about them is not that they require too little theoretical understanding but that they require too much. Moreover, much of the type of theory that is required is of the sort that is being developed within other disciplines in the university. At a time when there is a general outcry about the fragmentation and compartmentalization of knowledge and when attempts are being made to integrate various branches of study, a subject like that of education, which by its very nature is interdisciplinary, should surely be welcomed.

There is therefore no general reason deriving from our concept of a university for excluding educational studies from a university, and no reason why they should not be pursued by people without particularly practical concerns. But the fact is that most people are interested in education because of their practical concerns and, moreover, the disciplined pursuit of knowledge in this sphere is of vital importance both to the community in its need for the efficient transmission of knowledge and skill and to the individual in his attempt to make something of himself within the culture into which he has been born. In my view, a university should be outward looking towards the wider community and not just concerned with developing those theoretical pursuits which its inmates find fascinating. And practical problems have their own fascination. Witness the tradition at the Royal Society, going back to the 'invisible college' of the seventeenth century. Concern for the practical is too often confused with an instrumental attitude towards knowledge. In thinking, therefore, about the provision of educational studies in a university I would attach a great deal of weight to the predominantly practical interests of those who are likely to be attracted to them, namely the teaching profession.

A proper fusion between theory and practice, via the teaching profession, is essential to the health of educational theory. Psychologists, for instance, should not just fall back on some pure learning theory that they were taught in a pure university department and try to extrapolate it to the very different learning situation of the class-room; rather they should go out into the class-rooms with teachers and try to develop some theory that is relevant to the actual content, and conditions of learning, as well as to the state of mind of the learners. The benefit to practice is not always of an immediate sort; for only small segments of educational theory can be immediately applied in the way in which some physics can be applied to solve an engineering problem. Much of it has a more gradual effect in that it gradually transforms the teacher's view of his subject, the children and the context in which he is acting. And, of course, in a general sense no teacher, even the most practically minded one, approaches his tasks without theory. The only real question is whether the assumptions on which his practice is based are clear-headed or muddle-headed, based on evidence or on prejudice. Above all, nowadays the teacher needs the equipment to stand on his own feet, to preserve the remarkable autonomy which is granted to him in our educational system; for he is subject to all sorts of pressures emanating from popular magazines, publishing companies with gimmicks to sell, inspectors, and parents who are well aware that success at school is the royal road to ascent in the occupational structure. There is no longer any established tradition on which he can fall back in the face of such pressure; for in education there is now controversy about almost everything of importance — about the aims of education, about the curriculum, about teaching methods, about discipline, and about school organization. It is too late to damp down critical informed thought about education for fear that it may upset established traditions. They have already been upset. The urgent need is for teachers to be adequately equipped to deal with the fluid situation in which they are likely to find themselves.

187

More specifically, then, how should a university be concerned with educational studies in ways which can be linked with the practice of teaching? There is, first of all, the whole area of what are called 'foundation disciplines' such as philosophy, psychology, sociology, and history. The universities are necessarily centres where the people are working who are most likely to develop further understanding in these disciplines. Those who are working in applied fields such as philosophy of education, and educational psychology should be working in close association with those who are developing the disciplines in their purer form. The great importance of the BEd degree is not that the status of teachers has been enhanced by making a real degree available to teachers, but that it is providing a real opportunity for university and college of education people to get together in devising and teaching courses which are both intellectually rigorous and professionally relevant. To cut these links would be like pushing doctors out to train in hospitals without any connexion between them and universities via the teaching hospitals.

There is then the whole area of what are called main subjects such as English, geography and mathematics. The peculiarity of the teaching profession is not just that it has to master a whole range of skills, values and perspectives for which universities provide some kind of a theoretical basis. It also has to be initiated into a cultural heritage which is to provide the *content* of teaching. And universities are preeminently the centres of this cultural heritage, and it would be tragic if there were a huge gap between e.g. the literature, mathematics, history enjoyed by university students and that to which the teacher has access. There must be a close link between the teaching profession and the universities in this vast area. It is, to my mind, a scandalous state of affairs if mathematics and history mean one sort of thing to people in universities and another sort of thing to teachers who have not been trained in them. University teachers often complain about the rubbish that their children are taught in schools, just as teachers complain about the aridity and irrelevance to life of much of their university studies. Both should, perhaps, ponder on the lack of institutional links that makes these situations possible. It is this double type of connexion between the universities and the teaching profession — that of pedagogy and of content — that makes the teaching profession a unique one in its relation with the university. And it is impossible in the end to separate pedagogy from content; for learning is determined largely by what is to be learnt. This makes the much overworked distinction between 'academic' and 'professional' studies difficult to maintain.

I have argued so far for a close connexion between the universities and the teaching profession because of the long-term benefit to education in the schools. But benefits to the university itself as an institution could come about through an even closer association with the teaching profession.

In talking about the aims of the university as an institution I mentioned that of the general education of students. I myself think that to refuse to be concerned with this aim is to hide one's head in the sand; for the fact is that it is only the minority of students who will in fact go on to develop the frontiers of knowledge themselves. Too many courses are taught with this sort of end in view and those who flounder with highly specialized honours courses provide, as it were, the base of the pyramid which supports the few whose gifts lie in the direction of those of their teachers. It is arguable that, from the point of view of their own development, some of their time could be better spent on a more liberal type of education. This is particularly pertinent as it is becoming more and more apparent that a degree is no longer going to rank as a predictable passport to a good job.

A liberal education is of central importance in a society whose members can no longer accept some unitary ideal of life, whether provided by the church or by a political party. For its function is not just to present to the individual a cultural heritage in which he can try to make something of himself, but to introduce him to those studies, especially in the area of the humanities, which are likely to stimulate his capacity for choice, to make it more imaginative and better informed. For in a society like ours the individual has a wide area of discretion. It is not laid down what sort of man he should become. The onus is on him to find meaning in his life within an accepted framework of principles, such as

189

freedom, fairness and the consideration of people's interests, without which such individual discretion would degenerate into anarchy.

To teach subjects with this end in view is very different from teaching them with the dominant aim of training people who may later become university dons. Much more attention has to be paid to methods of teaching, to the diverse motivations of students, and to the values inherent in the different subjects on the curriculum. This sort of problem is one that is the stock-in-trade of the enlightened school-teacher and college of education lecturer, though it is too often seen just in the context of early school leavers, of awakening the interest of those who are so bored by what goes on at school that they either leave or break the place up. A joint approach to this sort of problem by university and school-teachers should prove beneficial to both. An example of this can be found in what is called the 'Education component' of main subjects in the London BEd degree. But this sort of co-operation is only possible if there are solid organic links between the universities, colleges of education and the teaching profession. There have to be real opportunities for representatives of each to work together on common tasks; for are not university teachers also teachers?

The universities and the autonomy of the teaching profession

There is a further reason why a close connexion with universities is essential to the teaching profession which is connected with its autonomy and hence with the autonomy of individual teachers. At the moment the curriculum of schools and colleges is not centrally determined or controlled. At the school level the headmaster, the governing body, and the local educational authority have some kind of say in it; but the situation is, formally speaking, so indeterminate that the headmaster in fact has a very large say. So also, indirectly, do the universities through the examination system, though, with the coming of the CSE, the teachers themselves now have a larger say in this — and rightly so. But the curriculum is not laid down in some central office as it is in many countries. Colleges of education, too, can shelter under the umbrella of their university Institute and have a major say in determining their own curriculum. In making changes they have mainly to convince colleagues in neighbouring colleges as well as university teachers. They do not have to convince government representatives on matters to do with the content of courses, though indirect pressure can come from this source through the control of finance. Maybe local teachers should be generally more involved in the business of training teachers. It should be regarded more as a shared responsibility than it is at the moment and institutional provision should be made for this. But this could easily be arranged within the existing framework, given that the cash were forthcoming to provide a proper teacher-tutor system.

It may, however, be put to the colleges that if the university umbrella is removed, they will now be free from a semi-mythical domination by universities. But who will move into this vacuum? Will they in fact be more autonomous? Or will the central and local government now in fact have much more say about what goes on in colleges if the university umbrella is furled? Will colleges have better protection from the peremptory demands of the Department of Education and Science and local authorities than they had when these demands had to come via Institute directors? Who in fact controls the policy of a body like the Schools Council, which was set up ostensibly to give teachers more opportunities for co-ordinating attempts to improve the school curriculum? Will the directors of the new regional bodies be very lonely men with no powerful institution like their local university to back them? Or will they in fact become high-ranking civil servants? And what will be the position of universities if they are offered some sop of academic links with colleges which are even further emasculated by the complete withdrawal of a major say in policy making and planning? And will this castration be canonized by ritualistic mumblings about the distinction between 'academic' and 'professional' concerns, which, in the case of teaching, is an impossible one to maintain?

Conclusion

In brief there are two main spheres in which a link between

191

the universities and the teaching profession is essential. First, in the sphere of pedagogy the universities are the centres where understanding is being advanced in disciplines such as philosophy, psychology, and sociology, which are essential to the development of educational theory. Second, in the sphere of content, such as mathematics, English and history, the universities are pre-eminently concerned with the development of those studies which must provide content to the school curriculum and to a liberal education. Organic links must exist between the universities and the teaching profession in both these spheres, and because of the inseparable connexion in learning between content and methods, it is ultimately impossible to make anything other than an arbitrary distinction between 'academic' and 'professional' components in this connexion.

Education in our society is not unified by any particular religious or political ideal. The nearest approach which is made to such a unifying ideal is the demand for autonomy, that each individual should develop the capacity for authentic choice and learn to make something of himself within a developing cultural heritage. The universities should provide one of the main growing points of this cultural heritage and should also provide an institutional safeguard for the freedom of schools and colleges from too much direction from central or local government.

© University of London, Institute of Education 1972

Index

Alcibiades, 121, 122
analysis, conceptual, 18—20, 170, 175
apprenticeship system, 136, 162—3
Aristotle, 23, 24, 89, 121
Arnold, M., 47
authority: reliance on, 104; of teacher, 137
autonomy: in individuals, 63—6, 79—84, 106, 192; of teaching profession, 39, 72, 190—1

Bacon, F., 162
BEd, 156, 158, 160, 181, 188, 190
Behaviourism, 170, 175
Bentham, J., 44
Bernstein, B.B., 165
Bloom's taxonomy, 175
boredom, relief of, 96—9
Bruner, J.S., 155, 174, 177

censorship in Plato, 124, 125, 130
classics teaching, 128, 136
colleges of education, 164—6, 173, 181, 188, 190
community education centres, 81
comprehensive education, 22, 40, 153
compulsory schooling, 80—1, CSE, 190
curriculum, 72—3, 143, 153, 190; courses, in teacher training, 153—7, 173, 185; spiral, in education course, 160; studies, 171—4, 185

democracy, 44, 132

de-schooling, 69, 84
development: child, 155—6, 173, 185; personal, 156
Dewey, J., 48, 83, 89, 115, 116, 170—1
discipline, 78, 144, 145, 167, 172, 183
δόξα, 123
Durkheim, E., 180

educated man, 10—14
education: as academic discipline, 167—80; aims of, 17—18; analysis of concept of, 3—21; argument for breadth in, 105—7; authority in, 83—4; child-centred, 144, 165; cognitive conditions of, 4—5, 8—10, 29—32, 87—8; compared with reform, 3—4, 18; economic considerations in, 36—8, 42, 71; etymology of word, 9—11; extrinsic objectives in, 35—8, 51—2, 72, 73—9, 84; historians of, 169, 171; imitation as element in, 83, 124, 162—3; instrumental view of, 18, 19, 26, 36—8, 90—5; justification of, 86—118; non-authoritarian, 79—84; non-instrumental view of, 14, 28, 95—114; in Plato, 119—32; play in, 124; processes of, 88—9; progressive, 171, 175; psychology of, 167, 169, 170, 172, 177, 187; quality in, 22—45; social principles in, 39—42; sociology of, 167, 169, 171, 172, 174; traditional, 152, 175; and training, distinction